The Ultimate Office Olympics

Hundreds of ways to pass the time at work without working!

Eric Saunders

FIREFLY BOOKS

A FIREFLY BOOK

Published by Firefly Books Ltd. 2010

First printing

Publisher Cataloging-in-Publication Data (U.S.)

Saunders, Eric.
 Ultimate Office Olympics : hundreds of ways to pass the time at work without working! / Eric Saunders.
 ISBN-13: 978-1-55407-622-2 (pbk.)
 ISBN-10: 1-55407-622-6 (pbk.)
 1. Puzzles. 2. Mathematical recreations. I. Title.
 793.73 dc22   GV1493.S286   2010

A CIP record for this book is available from Library and Archives Canada

Published in the United States by
Firefly Books (U.S.) Inc.
P.O. Box 1338, Ellicott Station
Buffalo, New York 14205

Published in Canada by
Firefly Books Ltd.
66 Leek Crescent
Richmond Hill, Ontario L4B 1H1

Printed in China

Puzzle compilation, typesetting and design by:

Eric Saunders
and
Diane Law

Domino Logic

What is the missing number?

(domino equations) = 18

(domino equations) = 20

(domino equations) = 4

(domino equations) = ?

Payday for Optimists

Finally you can buy that lovely new coat after saving for just three months!

Around the Water Cooler

- John from accounts is about to get fired.
- Liz in sales has gained 20lbs.
- The new intern looks like a walrus.
- The boss has his fly undone.

Clock Watching

How long is it until 5:30 p.m.?

Change the Word

Change boss to hush one word at a time

Boss

_____

_____

_____

Hush

Caught by the Boss

Asleep at your desk ☐

Taking the petty cash to buy a beer ☐

Gazing out the window during your appraisal meeting. ☐

Overheard mid-gossip ☐

Today's Target

1. Longer lunchbreak
2. Avoid Sue on reception
3. Unplug your phone

Sing While You Work

These are lyrics from a song about work. Can you name the song?

I was looking for a job and then I found a job

Wordwheel

Using only the letters in the wordwheel, you have ten minutes to find as many words as possible, none of which may be plurals, foreign words or proper nouns. Each word must be three letters or more, all must contain the central letter and letters can only be used once in every word.
There is at least one nine-letter word in the wheel.

Nine-letter word _____

Excuses for...

Leaving work early

_____

_____

_____

The Bottom Line

Plastic Monster Corporation buys 10,000 toy monsters for $1.20 and sells 8,000 of them for $2.00 a unit.

How much profit did the company make?

Thought for the Day

All paid jobs absorb and degrade the mind.
Aristotle (Ancient Greek Philosopher, 384 BC-322 BC)

Answers from previous page

Sing While You Work:
"Heaven Knows I'm Miserable Now"- The Smiths
Clock Watching = 4 hours and 50 minutes
Change the Word:
Boss, Bass, Bash, Mash, Hash, Hush
Domino Logic: Answer = 21
Multiply the total spots on the first domino by the total spots on the second, then subtract the total spots on the third domino.

Desktop Golf

1 ruler

Rules: Anything on your desk can become a golf hole. Empty paper cups, staple boxes, your in-tray or the paperclip holder. You could even be creative and use your shoes, your briefcase or a colleagues mouth.

Simply putt a rolled up paperball using a ruler. First to get around the course wins.

rolled up paper or sticky tape

Dice Man

Using three of the arithmetical signs +, −, X and ÷, can you achieve the correct total?

Payday for Pessimists

A 100 hour week and you're still in debt.

Exchange Rate

Can you find the value for each shape?

■ ■ ■ - ▲ ▲ = ●

● ● - ■ ■ ■ = ■

● ● ● - ■ ■ ■ ■ ■ ■ + 4 = ▲ ▲

Triangle = ?
Square = ?
Circle = ?

Get the Job

Can you unscramble the anagram to reveal the job title?

Fierce Foil Cop

Answer _____

Pick 'n' Mix

Describe your last job interview using the words below:

Harrowing
Joyful
Hopeless
Embarrassing
Encouraging
Insane

Answers from previous page

The Bottom Line: Answer = $4,000

Wordwheel nine-letter word: Oligopoly

Wastepaper Basketball

Instructions

1. Place a wastepasper basket on a filing cabinet.

2. Scrunch a piece of paper into a ball.
(For the best fun use your recent staff appraisal.)

3. Shoot at the basket.
(Other players can try to prevent a goal.)

4. The winner is the one who gets the most 'basket' goals.

Today's Greatest Achievement

Appearing sober and calm ☐

Grand Unified Theory ☐

Act of random kindness ☐

Which Movie Contains the Following Quote?

"If you've ever seen the look on somebody's face the day they finally get a job...they look like they could fly."

Work Face

Bonus Day

Top Five

Best songs for payday

1. _____
2. _____
3. _____
4. _____
5. _____

Mental Arithmetic

Your boss wants a $3.50 coffee, a $5.75 sandwich and a $2.95 fruit smoothie.

How much change will he get from $15.00?

Mind Games

Boss says...

"Let's do it!"

Boss means...

"You have to do it."

Unlikely Candidate

King _____

Answers from previous page

Get the Job: Answer = Police Officer

Dice Man: Answer = 3 x 5 - 3 ÷ 6 = 2

The Exchange Rate: Answer = Square = 4, Triangle = 2, Circle = 8

Top Ten

Sandwich Fillers

- Tomato ☐
- Salt Beef ☐
- Lettuce ☐
- Ham ☐
- Onions ☐
- Mozzarella ☐
- Egg ☐
- Peppers ☐
- Cheddar ☐
- Bacon ☐

Board Meeting Doodle

Lunchtime Sudoku

1	9			5			4	7
				6		1		
	2	8		7	4		9	
4	7	3			1			8
6								5
8			3			7	2	1
	3		8	1		6	5	
		4			2			
9	8			6			7	3

Place Your Bets

State of bank account:

Pleasingly full —/—

Nerve-wreckingly empty —/—

Frozen months ago by your bank —/—

Named and Shamed

Least eligible bachelor _____

Harboring dark secrets _____

Possible alien clone _____

Whatever You Do

Don't even think about any of the following:

Axe murderers

Crack in the bathroom ceiling

The length of your working day

Answers from previous page

Movie Quotes: Answer = Dave (1993)
Mental Arithmetic: Answer = $2.80

Around the World in Eighty Flights

1. Each competitor makes a paper airplane and a route around the office or factory floor is chosen.

2. Each player throws their craft from the starting line.

3. The next throw starts from where the airplane has landed.

4. Continue to throw in turn.

5. The winner is the one who reaches the finish line in the least throws.

(This competition is best scheduled for a day when the directors are out of town.)

Ways to Pass the Time

Eating ☐

Sleeping ☐

Waiting ☐

Design Your Own

Letter head:

Piggy Bank

While checking the petty cash drawer, you find that there is $252 in total. By coincidence there is an equal number of $20, $10, $5 and $1 dollar bills in the drawer.

How many of each type of bill are there?

Two-Word Horoscopes

Aries - you scoundrel

Taurus - dream on

Gemini - don't panic

Cancer - horny, hopeless

Leo - mystery man

Virgo - oops - again?

Libra - wake up!

Scorpio - colossal mess

Sagittarius - never mind

Capricorn - oh, God

Aquarius - why not?

Pisces - absurd attire

Answers from previous page

Lunchtime Sudoku:

1	9	6	2	5	8	3	4	7
7	4	5	6	9	3	1	8	2
3	2	8	1	7	4	5	9	6
4	7	3	5	2	1	9	6	8
6	1	2	9	8	7	4	3	5
8	5	9	3	4	6	7	2	1
2	3	7	8	1	9	6	5	4
5	6	4	7	3	2	8	1	9
9	8	1	4	6	5	2	7	3

Watching Paint Dry

The decorators are in the office.

On the first day they paint one third of the total area of the wall.

On the second day they paint one third of the remaining area.

On the third day they paint three quarters of the remaining area.

They now have an area of 20 square feet left to paint.
What is the total area of the wall?

Who Am I?

Can you work out which singer's name is hidden in the anagram below?

Honey With Snout

Work Face

New Colleague

Words to Impress Your Colleagues

Test yourself and expand your vocabulary.
Do you know the meaning of the word:

Vomitory?

My Next Career

Job Description _____

Salary _____

Hours _____

Today's Target

To make as many loud belching noises as possible without detection.

Brief Survival Guide

Sales Conference:

1. Mutate and mingle ☐

2. Identify crucial weakness ☐

3. Run for the hills ☐

Mass Hysterias

Today we are all going to...
Panic and faint because the reports are due in.

Answers from previous page

Piggy Bank: Answer = 7

What Color Was Your Parachute?

On a team building expedition, members of your office team have to go parachuting to learn to trust each other.

The total cost of the course to the company is $2,737, and the company is charged the same fee for each person.

You know that the number of people on the course is between 20 and 30.

How much was the fee per person?

Work Space

The Earth spins faster on its axis in September than it does in March.

Ridiculous Rules

In Los Angeles, California...
A city ordinance states that a $500 fine will be given to anyone who detonates a nuclear device within city limits.

Around the Water Cooler

The new boss is rubbish ☐

You're getting longer work hours ☐

A strike is imminent ☐

In the Calendar

What happened on November 10, 1775?

Top Five

Best songs for being made redundant:
1. _____
2. _____
3. _____
4. _____
5. _____

Answers from previous page

Watching Paint Dry: Answer = 180 square feet

Who Am I? Answer = Whitney Houston

Impress Your Colleagues: Answer = A vomitory is a passageway leading to a tier of seats in a theatre or stadium

Coffee Pot Snorkling

You will need a coffee pot with coffee in it and some dried beans.

1. Place the dried beans in the bottom of the pot of coffee. (NB. To avoid injury it should be fairly cool!)

2. Each player must try to retrieve the beans from the coffee pot using only the straw.

3. The winner is the one who collects the most beans.

Top Ten

Pen Colors:
- Red ☐
- Blue ☐
- Green ☐
- Gold ☐
- Silver ☐
- Orange ☐
- Purple ☐
- Black ☐
- Pink ☐
- Turquoise ☐

Guess the Phobia

A very common state of mind in most humans. Especially on Monday morning.

Ergophobia

The Bottom Line

Monkey Magic manufacture 6,000 gorilla suits for $8.50 a unit.
1,000 are given away as a promotion, the remainder are sold for $11.00 each.

How much profit did they make?

Morning Meditation

We are more often treacherous through weakness than through calculation.

Francois De La Rochefoucauld

Clock Watching

Lunch is at 1:00 p.m. How much longer?

Answers from previous page

In the Calendar: Answers = Birth of U.S. Marine Corps
What Color Was Your Parachute? Answer = $119 (for 23 people)

Design Your Own

[Mouse Mat drawing box]

Mouse Mat

Unlikely Candidate

Pope_____

Who Stole The Cheese?

At the lunch table we all draw lots.
Each time someone wins, they are given
x slices of cheese and y carrots.

The values for x and y never change.

At the end of the lot drawing, the cheese and
carrots are divided as follows:

Abby: Cheese 7, Carrots 8
Barney: Cheese 3, Carrots 4
Carol: Cheese 8, Carrots 12

Who Stole Who's Cheese?

Whatever You Do

Don't even think about any of the following:

They know that you lied on your CV

You badly need an argument to let off steam

It's a long way home

Get the Job

Unscramble the
anagram below to
find the job.

Cheater

Answer _____

Before They Were Famous

He's well known for his
crooning but what job did
Rod Stewart have before
he was famous?

Answer _____

Extinct Jobs

Whipping Boy:

In England in the 15th and 16th centuries. A
"whipping boy" was a boy who had grown up
with and was educated with the prince.
When the prince misbehaved the "whipping
boy" was punished instead because only a
king could punish a prince.

Answers from previous page

Guess the Phobia: Answer = fear of work
Clock Watching: Answer = 3 hours and 45
minutes
The Bottom Line: Answer = $4,000

Payday for Optimists

Still no pay rise but there's a good offer on beer down at the store.

Around the Water Cooler

- ■ You are certain to be fired
- ■ He is definitely fired
- ■ They are most probably all fired

Domino Logic

Can you work out the missing number and the reason why?

= 3

= 2

= 2

= ?

Change the Word

In six steps...

Cubed

_____

_____

_____

_____

Bonus

Today's Target

To see how many paperclips you can balance on your tongue.

Clock Watching

How long is it until the 7:00 a.m. alarm clock?

👁 Caught by the Boss

Gossiping about him ☐

Laughing at him ☐

Admitting you fancy him ☐

Answers from previous page

Get the Job: Answer = Teacher

Before They Were Famous: Rod Stewart was a grave digger

Who Stole the Cheese? Answer = Abby stole Carol's cheese

WORDWHEEL

Using only the letters in the Wordwheel, you have ten minutes to find as many words as possible, none of which may be plurals, foreign words or proper nouns. Each word must be three letters or more, all must contain the central letters and letters can only be used once in every word. There is at least one nine-letter word in the wheel.

Nine-letter word _____

Today's Target

To look incredulous and/or shocked by anything anyone says to you today

Thought For the Day

The best way to appreciate your job is to imagine yourself without one.

Oscar Wilde (Writer and Critic, 1854–1900)

The Bottom Line

HappyCom buys 4 companies for $10 million each. It sells the existing stock of the companies for $3 million each, then merges the companies and sells the new company for $25 million.

How much did it lose?

Answers from previous page

Domino Logic: Answer = 5 - Add the total spots on the first domino to the total spots on the second, then divide by the total spots on the third domino.

Clock Watching: Answer = 8 hours and 15 minutes

Change the Word:
Cubed, Cubes, Tubes, Tunes, Tones, Bones, Bonus

Dice Man

Using three of the arithmetical signs
+, -, × and ÷, can you achieve the
correct total?

Payday for Pessimists

A bonus at last but it won't pay for the
dent in your new car.

Boardroom Table Tennis

1. Make sure that there are no directors or
senior management around.

2. Go into the boardroom and place a row
of files along the desk.

3. Using folders for bats, hit the ball (either
scrunched up paper or a real ping pong ball)
back and forth along the length of the table.

You could even organize a tournament!

Lunchtime Sudoku

7			3				9	5
	5	9		1	2			
9			6			1		
8		6		4		2	3	
	6	2		3	9			
1	7		9		4	6		
3			2			8		
	8	1		6	7			
	6			4			5	2

Get the Job

Can you unscramble
the anagram below
to get the job title?

Impart Cash

Answer _____

Pick 'n' Mix

Choose 3 words to plan
your lunch order

Boring   Chic

Outlandish   Minimal

Superior   Nouvelle

Low Fat   Take-away

Booze-fest   Greasy

Answers from previous page

Wordwheel nine-letter word = Automaton

The Bottom Line: Answer = $3 million

Top Ten

Leaving Bouquets:

- Daisies ☐
- Tulips ☐
- Roses ☐
- Poppies ☐
- Daffodils ☐
- Buttercups ☐
- Hyacinths ☐
- Sunflowers ☐
- Pansies ☐
- Bluebells ☐

Board Meeting Doodle

Place Your Bets

Contents of desk drawer:

3 novelty ties	—/—
1 unidentifiable foodstuff	—/—
Lost chequebook and dust	—/—

Named and Shamed

Least Likely To Succeed _____

Suspected Enemy Agent _____

Most Insipid Demeanour _____

The Bottom Line

HousesForEveryoneCorps buys 5,000 condos for $100,000 each. The price falls by 10% and they sell half the units at a loss. Now the price rises by 20% and they sell the other half at a profit.

Have they made an overall loss or profit?

Whatever You Do

Don't even think about any of the following:

You are being watched by hidden cameras

Your computer has been hacked into

You are thinking that you're paranoid

Answers from previous page

Lunchtime Sudoku:

Get the Job:

Answer = pharmacist

Dice Man:

Answer = 3 x 1 + 5 ÷ 2 = 4

6	7	1	8	3	2	4	9	5
3	4	5	9	7	1	2	6	8
8	9	2	4	6	5	3	1	7
9	8	7	6	1	4	5	2	3
4	5	6	2	8	3	9	7	1
2	1	3	7	5	9	8	4	6
1	3	4	5	2	7	6	8	9
5	2	8	1	9	6	7	3	4
7	6	9	3	4	8	1	5	2

Ways to Pass the Time

Chattering ☐
Laughing ☐
Worrying ☐

Design Your Own

Desktop photo arrangement

Office Mini-Doughnut Eating Competition

Tom eats an average of 3 doughnuts a minute for the first 10 minutes of the competition. By the end of the half hour competition, his average has slowed down to 2.5 doughnuts a minute.

How many doughnuts did he eat in the last twenty minutes?

Piggy Bank

At the bar, the till starts out empty and ends up with $4,200 in it.

A total of 240 bottles were sold.

A quarter of the bottles sold were champagne.

Champagne costs twice as much as wine.

How much does a bottle of wine cost?

Two-Word Horoscopes

Aries - no hope
Taurus - bad luck
Gemini - good news
Cancer - what now?
Leo - ignore them
Virgo - at last!

Libra - surf's up
Scorpio - you're serious?
Sagittarius - not now...
Capricorn - party time
Aquarius - so unfair!
Pisces - as usual

Answers from previous page

The Bottom Line: Answer = A loss ($5 million, because the final price is only 8% higher than the starting price)

Who Am I?

What famous couple is contained in the anagram below?

A Bankcard Ah Victim Devoid

Watching Paint Dry

The decorators are in the office.

On the wall you find the following series of letters painted on the panels they are planning on decorating.

O T T F F S S E N T   What is the next letter?

Work Face

Finance Meeting

Words to Impress Your Colleagues

Test yourself and expand your vocabulary
Do you know the meaning of the word:

Yeuk?

Sing While You Work

These lyrics are from a song about work.
Can you guess the song?

Everyone's hoping it'll all work out,
Everyone's waiting they're holding out.

Today's Target

To not quite complete any sentence you utter all day, or in other words...

Brief Survival Guide

New Area Manager:

Play dead

Cultivate glassy stare

Machete madness

Mass Hysterias

Today we are all going to:

Carry umbrellas in case the sky falls down.

Answers to previous page

Office Mini-Doughnut Eating: Answer = 45 doughnuts
Piggy Bank: Answer = $14.00

Who Bought The Cheese?

Abby, Barney and Carol go out shopping together.

The meat costs twice as much as the cheese, the cheese costs twice as much as the carrots. Altogether, they spend $21.00

Abby starts out with $10.00 and ends up with $7.00

Carol starts with no money, borrows $10.00 from Barney and ends up with $4.00

Barney starts out with $30.00 and ends up with $1.00 more than Abby

Who bought the cheese?

Work Space

The planet Venus spins the opposite way from the other planets.

Around the Water Cooler

You should have phoned in sick

She has phoned in sick

They are both off sick together!

Ridiculous Rules

In the United Kingdom it is illegal to die in the Houses of Parliament. It also could be regarded an act of treason to place a postage stamp bearing the British king or queen's image upside-down.

In the Calendar

In what year was the FBI founded?

Top Five

Best songs for being late for work:

1. _____

2. _____

3. _____

4. _____

5. _____

Answers from previous page

Watching Paint Dry: Answer = E (For "Eleven". Oddly, the decorators have painted the first letter of each number, starting from One).

Who Am I? Answer = David and Victoria Beckham

Words: yeuk is a 15th century Middle English word used by the Scots meaning "to itch."

Sing While You Work: Answer = *Working for the Weekend* Loverboy

Top Ten

Work Clothes:

- Shirt ☐
- Sweater ☐
- Vest ☐
- Waistcoat ☐
- Blouse ☐
- Pullover ☐
- T-shirt ☐
- Tank Top ☐
- Jacket ☐
- Cardigan ☐

Notice Board Darts

You may have to bring in your own darts for this one.

1. Give a numeric value to every item on your notice board. (For example a social event may score 10 and a dreaded meeting score only 1).
2. Organize yourselves into two teams and throw the darts at the notice board.
3. Set a number of points that will need to be won.
4. The team who reaches that score first wins.

Guess the Phobia

You probably suffer from this on mornings when you're late:

Scopophobia

Clock Watching

The server is off until 4:20 p.m. How long do you have to wait?

Morning Meditation

I am a part of all that I have met.

Alfred Lord Tennyson

The Bottom Line

Bling Bonanza Stores buys 1,000 glamtastic sequinned tops for $12.00 each. They sell 200 for $100 each, then sell off the surplus stock for $5.00 in the sale.

How much profit did they make?

Answers from previous page

Who Bought the Cheese?
Answer = Carol bought the cheese.

In the Calendar: Answer = 1908

The One-Minute Preacher

Here is a well-known proverb with the vowels (and "y"s and punctuation) removed and the letters put into groups of three.

Can you decipher it?

JCK FLL TRD SMS TRF NN

Design Your Own
Interview Tie

Morning Meditation

Work spares us from three evils: boredom, vice, and need.

Voltaire (French Philosopher 1694-1778)

Change the Word

In 5 steps:

Risk

_____

_____

_____

Wage

Place Your Bets

Tonights drinks tally:

1 dry martini, 1 French wine   —/—

4 beers, 2 Scotch whiskeys   —/—

7 spritzers, ??? Colombian tequilas —/—

Named and Shamed

Needing Personality Infusion _____
Most Cloying Couple _____
Too Innocent To Be True _____

Unlikely Candidate

World Leader _____

Mass Hysterias	In the Calendar

Today we are all going to:

Cry endlessly about the new project.

What happened on March 17, 1776?

Answers from previous page

The Bottom Line: Answer = $12,000

Clock Watching: Answer = 3 hours and 20 minutes

Guess the Phobia: Answer = fear of being looked at.

The One-Minute Magician

1. Think of a number between 2 and 9.

2. Multiply the number by 9.

3. Add the digits of your result together.

4. Multiply this number by 10.

5. Add your original number to the result.

6. Write this number down somewhere secret.

I know what number you were thinking of!
(see answer)

   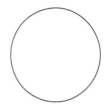

Work Face

Promotion

Unlikely Candidate

Love Interest
_____

Whatever You Do

Don't even think about any of the following:

Moldy fruit

Subcutaneous eruptions

Coming home after the clock strikes twelve

Get the Job

Unscramble the anagram below to find the job.

Idle Rub

Answer _____

Before They Were Famous

Michael Dell of Dell Computers fame wasn't always so loftily employed. Do you know what his first job was?

Answer _____

Extinct Jobs

Groom of the Stool:

The "Groom of the Stool" was a male servant in the household of an English monarch who, presided over the toilet activities during royal excretion. What he actually did was clean the monarch's anus after defecation.

Answers from previous page:

Change the Word: Risk, Rise, Ride, Wide, Wade, Wage

The One-Minute Preacher: Answer = Jack of all trades, master of none

In the Calendar: Answer = The British evacuate Boston

Domino Logic

What is the missing number?

   = 8

 = 2

 = 4

 = ?

Clock Watching

The meeting finishes at 3:30 p.m.
How much longer?

Today's Target

1. To unplug the phone and spy on your boss
2. To shred the evidence

Change the Word

Change cares to happy one word at a time

Cares

_____

_____

_____

_____

Happy

Payday for Optimists

Almost enough money now for a new pair of shoes, only one more month of going to work with wet feet.

Around the Water Cooler Today:

- [ ] Sally in sales is having an affair
- [ ] Someone has stolen the petty cash
- [ ] Everyone is on drugs
- [ ] There's an alcoholic in the building

Sing While You Work

These are lyrics from a song about work. Can you name the song?

They hurt you at home and they hit you at school,
They hate you if you're clever and they despise a fool.

Answers from previous page

The One-Minute Magician: Answer = Ignore the first digit of the result, the second digit is your original number.

Before They Were Famous: Answer = Michael Dell was a dishwasher

Get the Job: Answer = builder

Wordwheel

Using only the letters in the wordwheel, you have ten minutes to find as many words as possible, none of which may be plurals, foreign words or proper nouns. Each word must be three letters or more, all must contain the central letter and letters can only be used once in every word.
There is at least one nine-letter word in the wheel.

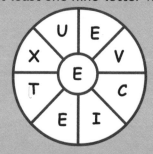

Nine-letter word _____

Excuses for...

Two weeks at the beach.

_____

_____

_____

Work Face

Office Romance

The Bottom Line

In Jiggery Pokery Restaurants, the dishwashers are paid $9.00 an hour, the chefs $12.00 an hour, and the waiters $10.00 an hour. If two waiters, two chefs and one dishwasher work a four hour shift, how much is the wage bill for the shift?

Thought for the Day

The most important job is not to be governor, or first lady in my case.

George W. Bush (43rd U.S. President)

Answers from previous page

Sing While You Work: Answer = *Working Class Hero* - John Lennon

Clock Watching: Answer = 3 hours and 50 minutes

Cares, Cards, Carps, Harps, Harpy, Happy

Domino Logic: Answer = 2

(Add the total spots on the left hand side of the dominos and subtract by the total spots on the right hand side.)

Ruler Relay

You will need one ruler per team:

1. Create a course around the office.

2. Organize yourselves into teams and agree on swap over relay points along the course.

3. Each player races against the other team and the ruler should be handed over at the relay points.

4. The winner is the first to cross the finish line.

Dice Man

Using three of the arithmetical signs +, −, X and ÷, can you achieve the correct total?

Payday for Pessimists

You've got a full week's overtime pay but it's raining and you can't be bothered to go shopping.

Lunchtime Sudoku

	1	4		7			9	2
		8		6				
	9			3	1		5	7
		1			9	3	6	2
		7				5		
9	2	8	3			1		
1	6		8	2			4	
					7			3
	4	3		5		2	8	

Get the Job

Can you unscramble the anagram to reveal the job title?

Main Lam

Answer _____

Pick 'n' Mix

Your evening in:

Violent   Epic

Sensual   Worthy

Comedy   Pointless

Foreign   Gothic

Drama   Spectacular

Answers from previous page

The Bottom Line: Answer = $212.00

Wordwheel nine-letter word:
Answer = Executive

The One-Minute Preacher

Here is a well-known proverb with the vowels (and "y"s and punctuation) removed and the letters put into groups of three.

Can you decipher it?

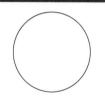

DNT PTL LRG GSN NBS KT

Today's Greatest Achievement

Not panicking ▪

Saving universe (again) ▪

Getting out of bed ▪

Which Movie Contains the Following Quote?

"Judges, lawyers, cops, politicians. They stop bringing dope into this country, about a hundred thousand people are going to be out of a job."

Work Face

Weary

Top Five

Best songs for after work drinks:

1. _____
2. _____
3. _____
4. _____
5. _____

Brain Teasers

Which artist released an album and movie under the same title of *Get Rich Or Die Tryin`*?

Answers from previous page

Mind Games

Boss says:
"I am very open to other viewpoints."

Boss means:
"Things will actually be done my way."

Unlikely Candidate

Head of the FBI

_____

Lunchtime Sudoku: Answer =

3	1	4	5	7	8	9	2	6
8	7	5	6	9	2	4	3	1
2	9	6	4	3	1	8	5	7
4	5	1	7	8	9	3	6	2
6	3	7	2	1	4	5	9	8
9	2	8	3	6	5	1	7	4
1	6	9	8	2	3	7	4	5
5	8	2	9	4	7	6	1	3
7	4	3	1	5	6	2	8	9

Get the Job:
Answer = Mailman

Dice Man:
Answer = 6 ÷ 3 x 4 - 6 = 2

Top Ten

After Work Drinks

Whisky ☐
Gin ☐
Lager ☐
Vodka ☐
Beer ☐
Wine ☐
Sherry ☐
Champagne ☐
Tequila ☐
Vermouth ☐

Board Meeting Doodle

The Bottom Line

Dipsywoo.com have 100 staff on an average income of $20,000 a year plus 5 managers on $300,000 a year. They are making a loss of $300,000 a year.

How many staff do they have to lay off to make up for the loss next year?

Place Your Bets

_____'s outfit today will be:

Smart, sober, sensible   __/__

Crude, crazy, crass   __/__

Wacky, weird, why?   __/__

Named and Shamed

Worst dressed   _____

Bad hair day   _____

Bad fat day   _____

Whatever You Do

Don't even think about any of the following:

Nails on a blackboard

Polystyrene being rubbed

Damp patch in the bedroom

Answers from previous page

The One-Minute Preacher: Answer = Don't put all your eggs in one basket

Movie Quote: Answer = *American Gangster* (2007)

Brain Teaser: Answer = 50 Cent

Diving for Victory

Set up a diving board, by using a heavy weight to anchor a ruler, which protrudes over the side of a desk.

Fill a washing up bowl with water and place it below the diving board.

Each competitor must build a miniature diver, out of paper, staples, rubber bands and any other pieces of office paraphernalia.

Ways to Pass the Time

Singing ☐

Dancing ☐

Shouting ☐

Design Your Own

Coffee mug:

Piggy Bank

A restaurant has a slow start to a thirty day month, averaging $2,000 in the first ten days.

After that things pick up and at the end of the month, the average daily take for the thirty days is $2,200.

What was the average take in the last twenty days of the month?

Two-Word Horoscopes

Aries - Big deal

Taurus - Watch out

Gemini - No fun

Cancer - Lost causes

Leo - Sorry tales

Virgo - New admirer

Libra - Lovely dinner

Scorpio - Better directions

Sagittarius - No takers

Capricorn - Go on!

Aquarius - Big trouble

Pisces - Bad business

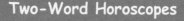

Answers from previous page

The Bottom Line: Answer =15 ordinary staff or 1 manager. Tricky choice, hmm...

Watching Paint Dry

The decorators are in the office. They have got confused about which colors they are supposed to be using.

Can you find five different colors in the anagram below?

WERE ON A RYE ROLL GLEE BED GUN

Who Am I?

Can you work out which singer's name is hidden in the anagram below?

Archangel Zeds Wronger

Work Face

Broken Computer

Words to Impress Your Colleagues

Test yourself and expand your vocabulary.
Do you know the meaning of the word:

Cacogen?

My Next Mistake

What _____

Why _____

Where _____

Today's Target

To speak only in rhyming couplets even on the phone without detection.

Brief Survival Guide

New Assistant:

1. Be vague ☐

2. Be scary ☐

3. Hide ☐

Mass Hysterias

Today we are all going to...

Start internet rumors about our business rivals.

Answers from previous page

Piggy Bank: Answer = $2,300

Lunchtime Synchronized Swimming

Split the group into teams of two or more swimmers. The office floor represents the pool, while the desktops represent the level of the water.

Each team must perform a synchronized routine, remember to hold their breath while under the "water," and smile, smile, smile while they are above the water.

Either an independent team of judges, or all the other competitors hold up cards with points from 1 to 10.

The team with the most points is the winner, and is awarded a victory bouquet.

Work Space

The planets Mercury and Venus are the only planets in our solar system that don't have moons.

Ridiculous Rules

In Singapore, it is illegal to come within 50 meters of a pedestrian crossing marker on any street.

What They Said

It's a recession when your neighbor loses his job; it's a depression when you lose yours.

Harry S Truman
(33rd President of the United States)

In the Calendar

What happened on June 20, 1863?

Top Five

Best songs for getting out of bed:
1. _____
2. _____
3. _____
4. _____
5. _____

Answers from previous page

Watching Paint Dry: Answer = Red Blue Green Orange Yellow

Who Am I? Answer = Arnold Schwarzenegger

Impress Your Colleagues: Answer = A cacogen is an antisocial person.

Sticky Bun Dartboard

Set up a target on the wall (or whiteboard):

Buy a bag of sticky buns.

Each competitor has two buns to start with.

Competitors take turns to throw their buns at the target.

Points (as per the target scores) are earned for any buns that stick to the target for a count of three.

Turns continue until no competitor has a bun left that will stick.

Buns can be used more than once.

Target values: 16, 10, 5, 25, 50, 20, 1, 12, 8

Top Ten

Shopfloor Footwear:

- Sandals ☐
- Loafers ☐
- Boots ☐
- Wellies ☐
- Flip-flops ☐
- Trainers ☐
- Pumps ☐
- Roller skates ☐
- Baseball boots ☐
- Ballet shoes ☐

Guess the Phobia

You may get this when your bank statements arrive in the mail:

Arithmophobia

The Bottom Line

GrowYourHairBack.com has offered a full money back guarantee on its Jojoba and Gumnut Hair Restorer. It makes 10,000 bottles for $3.00, sells them all at $30.00, but 1,000 customers ask for their money back.

What is the profit?

Answers from previous page

In the Calendar: Answer = West Virginia enters the Union in America.

Morning Meditation

Begin at the beginning and go on till you come to the end; then stop.

Lewis Carrol

Clock Watching

Coffee break is at 11:15 a.m. How much longer?

Design Your Own

Reception

Unlikely Candidate

Professor_____

Where Is My Cheese?

▲ ■ ●

Picture these moves in your head, and keep careful track.
Swap the triangle with the circle.
Swap the blue shape with the red shape.
Put the cheese inside the right hand box.
Swap the triangle with the circle.
Swap the blue shape with the red shape.
Move the cheese to the box in the middle.
Swap the triangle with the circle.
Swap the blue shape with the red shape.
Is the cheese on the left, on the right, or in the middle?

Whatever You Do

Don't even think about any of the following:

Your bank balance that you've been ignoring

Your overstuffed in-tray

That phone message that you were supposed to have replied to last week

Get the Job

Unscramble the anagram below to find the job.

Assassin Let Sat

Answer _____

Before They Were Famous

This hip-hop star is now a multi-millionaire but what did Sean Combs (P Diddy) do before he was famous?

Answer _____

Extinct Jobs

Knocker-Up:

In England and Ireland in the 1800's, a "knocker-up's" job was to rouse sleeping people so they could get to work on time. They would knock on upper windows with a long stick until the people inside were awake. People paid them a few pennies a week each.

Answers from previous page

Guess the Phobia: Answer = Fear of numbers.

Clock Watching: Answer = 1 hour and 55 minutes

The Bottom Line: Answer = $240,000

Payday for Optimists

Nice summer evening ... maybe one day you'll be able to go to that expensive new restaurant with the lovely views.

Around the Water Cooler

- ■ You are deleriously happy
- ■ He is absolutely gutted
- ■ They are very definitely pleased

Domino Logic

Can you work out the missing number and the reason why?

[domino] [domino] [domino] = 8

[domino] [domino] [domino] = 8

[domino] [domino] [domino] = 13

[domino] [domino] [domino] = ?

Change the Word

In six steps...

Mind

____

____

____

____

____

Task

Today's Target

To infect your colleagues with a sense of profound ennui and disdain for all of modern life.

Clock Watching

The late shift ends at 9:30 p.m. How long until then?

👁 Caught by the Boss

Shredding the evidence ☐

Photocopying the evidence ☐

Calling the authorities ☐

Answers from previous page

Where is My Cheese? Answer = On the right, in the green circle.

Get the Job: Answer = Sales Assistant

Before They Were Famous: Sean Combs was a paper boy.

WORDWHEEL

Using only the letters in the Wordwheel, you have ten minutes to find as many words as possible, none of which may be plurals, foreign words or proper nouns. Each word must be three letters or more, all must contain the central letters and letters can only be used once in every word. There is at least one nine-letter word in the wheel.

Nine-letter word _____

Thought For the Day

It's just a job. Grass grows, birds fly, waves pound the sand. I beat people up.

Muhammad Ali (Boxer and Activist)

The Bottom Line

Daisy Dunderhead has been paid a $250,000 advance for her kiss and tell memoir. Each copy of the book sells for $12.50 and she is on a 10% royalty.

How many copies does the Blurb Publishing Company have to sell before her advance is earned out?

Answers from previous page

Domino Logic: Answer = 7 = Divide the left hand side of each domino by the right hand side, then add the results together.

Clock Watching: Answer = 7 hours and 15 minutes

Change the Word:
Mind, Mine, Mane, Bane, Bank, Tank, Task

Dice Man

Using three of the arithmetical signs +, -, × and ÷, can you achieve the correct total?

Ball Point Pen Javelin

1. Clear an area designated as the drop landing site.

2. Each player throws his or her ballpoint pen into the drop zone.

3. The winner is the player who throws their pen the furthest.

Payday for Pessimists

An extra $10,000 per year in your new job, but the suit they make you wear keeps itching.

Lunchtime Sudoku

3	7				1		2	9
	9			2			4	
	1	4	6				3	8
5		2	8	7				
		6				8		
			9	3	5			4
	2	1			4	7	5	
	5			1			9	
7	6		5				1	8

Get the Job

Can you unscramble the anagram below to get the job title?

Deer Sing

Answer _____

Pick 'n' Mix

Choose 3 words to plan your new job title:

Executive   President

Manager   Information

Logistics   Household

Director   Structures

Dogsbody   Control

Answers from previous page

Wordwheel nine-letter word = Marketing

The Bottom Line: Answer = 200,000 copies

Top Ten

Coffee Flavors:

Chocolate ☐
Vanilla ☐
Strawberry ☐
Mint ☐
Mocha ☐
Fudge ☐
Raspberry ☐
Hazelnut ☐
Choc chip ☐
Toffee ☐

Board Meeting Doodle

Place Your Bets

Beneath the desk_____ is wearing:

Comedy duck feet —/—

Fetching pink sarong —/—

Ankle cuffs, tagging device —/—

Named and Shamed

Overrated _____

Overblown _____

Over _____

The One-Minute Comedian

Here is a corny joke with the vowels (and "y"s and punctuation) removed and the letters put into groups of three. Can you decipher it?

MYD GSG TNN SHW
DST SML LTR RBL

Whatever You Do

Don't even think about any of the following:

Your urgently required tax forms

Metal tooth fillings in the stapler

Going out with that makeup plastered on your face

Answers from previous page

Lunchtime Sudoku:

Get the Job:

Answer = Designer

Dice Man:

Answer = 1 + 6 - 3 ÷ 2 = 2

3	7	5	4	8	1	6	2	9
6	9	8	3	2	7	1	4	5
2	1	4	6	5	9	3	8	7
5	4	2	8	7	6	9	3	1
9	3	6	1	4	5	8	7	2
1	8	7	2	9	3	5	6	4
8	2	1	9	6	4	7	5	3
4	5	3	7	1	8	2	9	6
7	6	9	5	3	2	4	1	8

Ways to Pass the Time

Walking ☐

Jumping ☐

Skipping ☐

Design Your Own

Logo

The One-Minute Zookeeper

A chimpanzee costs $100

A giraffe costs $70

An alligator costs $90

How much should you expect to pay for a tiger?

Brain Teaser

What is the capital of the Caribbean island of Grenada?

Answer _____

Piggy Bank

In a restaurant one night, the average man spends $7 more than the average woman.

The total amount spent by women is $50 more than the total amount spent by men.

There were 30 men in the restaurant that night, and they spent a total of $810.

How many women were there?

Two-Word Horoscopes

Aries - Two times?   Libra - Little prayer

Taurus - Big money   Scorpio - Will travel

Gemini - No vacancy   Sagittarius - Not sure?...

Cancer - Nice try!   Capricorn - Better food

Leo - Evil hears   Aquarius - Good mending

Virgo - Naughty you   Pisces - The rest?

Answers from previous page

The One-Minute Comedian: Answer = My dog has no nose. How does it smell? Terrible.

Who Am I?

Which well-known actor is contained in the anagram below?

Minstrel Wail Ha

Work Face

Liquid Lunch

Watching Paint Dry

The decorators are in the office.

They have painted the following letters on the wall.

L A K E

A

K

E

Can you find three more words to complete a word square, where the words read the same across and down the grid? The words must be proper words.

Words to Impress Your Colleagues

Test yourself and expand your vocabulary

Do you know the meaning of the word:

Lamprophony?

Sing While You Work

These lyrics are from a song about work. Can you guess the song?

All of your family had to kill to survive, and they're still waitin' for their big day to arrive.

Today's Target

Just act natural for now. We will contact you again when the end is near

Brief Survival Guide

Tax man:

Invisible ink

Pretensions of honesty

Off shore bank account

Mass Hysterias

Today we are all going to:

Meow like possessed cats and walk on all fours.

Answers from previous page

The One-Minute Zookeeper: Answer = $50 - $10 per letter
Piggy Bank: Answer = 43
Brain Teaser: Answer = St. Georges

What Color Was Your Parachute?

Abby, Barney and Carol go shopping for adventure gear.

Each buys a parachute, a canoe and a lifejacket.

Altogether they buy three blue items, three green and three red.

Each one buys three items of different colors.

Abby buys a green canoe, Barney a blue lifejacket and Carol doesn't buy a green canoe.

What color is Abby's parachute?

Around the Water Cooler

Nobody knows what's going on ▪

He'll find out what's going on ▪

She knows what's going on ▪

Ridiculous Rules

In the United Kingdom, a pregnant woman can legally relieve herself anywhere she wants. Even outside in public places. If she's not pregnant it is illegal.

In the Calendar

When was Iraq admitted into the League of Nations, winning independence from British rule?

Top Five

Best songs for a spring morning:

1. _____
2. _____
3. _____
4. _____
5. _____

Printer Daredevil Challenge

If your office has a shared printer, the challenge is as follows:

Loiter by the printer. Whenever anyone prints a document, attempt to grab it before they can see it, saying, "This one's mine", (or similar excuses).

If you get caught, the challenge is over. Put their document in the recycling, then repeat, until you achieve one of the following point winning results:

Someone kicks the photocopier and breaks it—10 points

A co-worker loses their temper and uses bad language—20 points

The IT department are called in to explain the fault—5 points

Two of your co-workers have an argument about who's been taking their documents—15 points.

You get fired—25 points.

(Warning: this challenge is only for the bravest, and those who can afford to lose their jobs.)

Guess the Phobia

The company directors definitely don't suffer from this:

Chrematophobia

The Bottom Line

The CompulsoryFun restaurant chain gives away 1,000 free child meals, each costing it $5. As a result of the promotion it sells 2,500 adult meals, each at a profit of $8.

How much profit did the promotion generate?

Clock Watching

The afternoon break is at 3:45 p.m. How long do you have to wait?

Morning Meditation

Believe those who are seeking the truth. Doubt those who find it.

Andre Gide

Answers from previous page

What Color Was Your Parachute?
Answer = Blue

In the Calendar: Answer = October 3, 1932

The One-Minute Comedian

Here is a corny joke with the vowels (and "y"s and punctuation) removed and the letters put into groups of three.
Can you decipher it?

WHD DTH CHC KNC RSS THR DTG TTT HTH RSD

Design Your Own

Lunchtime Banquet

Morning Meditation

Even a clock that does not work is right twice a day.

Polish proverb

Change the Word

In 5 steps:

Moan

_____

_____

_____

_____

Help

Place Your Bets

The train home will be:

Punctual, empty, strangely calm — —/—

Late, sweaty, full of lunatics — —/—

Broken down, kaput, not coming — —/—

Named and Shamed

Biggest bottom _____

Overdone fake tan _____

Over bleached blonde _____

Unlikely Candidate

Rock Star _____

Mass Hysterias

Today we are all going to:

Keep one eye out for the manager that is roaming the area.

In the Calendar

What happened on November 24, 1859?

Answers from previous page

The Bottom Line: Answer = $15,000

Clock Watching: Answer = 2 hours and 55 minutes

Guess the Phobia: Answer = Fear of money

Getting in Shape

How many times can this shape

be positioned in this shape

in such a way that the squares exactly overlap?

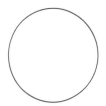
Whatever You Do

Don't even think about any of the following:

The smell of rotting meat

Paper cuts in your fingers

Wearing that suit with those shoes

Get the Job

Unscramble the anagram below to find the job.

Brush Pile

Answer _____

Before They Were Famous

Pol Pot is best known as a world famous war criminal, but what did he do before his military career?

Answer _____

Extinct Jobs

Toad Doctor:

In 19th century England, "Toad Doctors" were people who performed a folk-magic type medicine thought to counteract witches' curses. They attempted to cure the sick by placing a live toad, or the leg of one, in a muslin bag and hanging it around the sick person's neck.

Answers from previous page:

Change word: Moan, Loan, Lean, Leap, Heap, Help
The One-Minute Comedian: Answer = Why did the chicken cross the road? To get to the other side.
In the Calendar: Answer = Darwin's Origin of Species was published.

Domino Logic

What is the missing number?

Payday for Optimists

Another year without a bonus.
Still, you are on a diet anyway.

Breaktime Brain Teasers

Which U.S. rapper died on September 13th 1996 after being shot in a drive-by shooting after watchin Mike Tyson's comeback fight 7 days earlier?

Clock Watching

How long is it until 5:30 p.m.?

Today's Target

To erect a forcefield around your desk using only rubber bands, silver foil and string.

Change the Word

Change Melt to Safe in 6 steps

Melt
_____
_____
_____
_____
_____
Safe

Sing While You Work

These are lyrics from a song about work. Can you name the song?

Tumble outta bed
And stumble to the kitchen
Pour myself a cup of ambition

Answers from previous page

Getting in Shape: Answer = 12

Before They Were Famous: Answer = Pol Pot was a school teacher.

Get the Job: Answer = Publisher

Wordwheel

Using only the letters in the wordwheel, you have ten minutes to find as many words as possible, none of which may be plurals, foreign words or proper nouns. Each word must be three letters or more, all must contain the central letter and letters can only be used once in every word.

There is at least one nine-letter word in the wheel.

Nine-letter word _____

The Bottom Line

It takes me 15 hours to make a matchstick cathedral, and I can then sell it for $50. Meanwhile, it takes me 25 hours to make a matchstick replica of the Titanic, which I can sell for $65.

Which one is more profitable per hour?

Thought for the Day

If you can do a half-assed job of anything, you're a one-eyed man in a kingdom of the blind.

Kurt Vonnegut, Jr. (American Writer)

Answers from previous page

Sing While You Work: Answer = *9 to 5* Dolly Parton
Clock Watching: Answer = 7 hours and 40 minutes.   Change the Word: Answer = Melt, Belt, Bell, Ball, Bale, Sale, Safe
Domino Logic: Answer = 8
(Divide the total spots on the first domino by the total spots on the second domino, then add the total spots on the third.)
Breaktime Brainteasers: Answer = Tupac Shakur

Ruler Slingshot

You will need one ruler and elastic band per person:

1. Designate a waste paper bin as a goal.

2. Stretch an elastic band around the top of the ruler.

3. Screw up a piece of paper to use as a ball. And aim it at the bin using the ruler and elastic band as a slingshot.

4. The winner is the one who scores the most "goals."

Dice Man

Using three of the arithmetical signs +, −, X and ÷, can you achieve the correct total?

Payday for Pessimists

A whole week off on full pay! But you've been given community service for breaking a window.

Lunchtime Sudoku

1				7	3	8	2	
	2				8		9	1
4		6			9			
9		2			4		6	
		4	5		1	3		
	7		9			2		5
			3			5		7
5	3		1				8	
	1	7	8	6				4

Get the Job

Can you unscramble the anagram to reveal the job title?

Triode

Answer _____

Pick 'n' Mix

The new receptionists's style:

Ridiculous   Smart

Cathartic   Cosmic

Classic   Abstract

New-wave   Uber-

Puritan   Dull

Answers from previous page

The Bottom Line: Answer = The cathedral

Wordwheel nine-letter word: Incentive

The One-Minute Zookeeper

In the zoo there are:

Three flamingos

One skunk

Four bald eagles

Four kangaroos

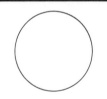

How many owls do
you think there might be?

Today's Greatest Achievement

Undermining Boss's Scheme

New Sandwich Filling

Nobel Nomination

Which Movie Contains the Following Quote?

*"There is something you should
understand about the way I work.
When you need me but do not want me,
then I'll stay. When you want me but
no longer need me, then I have to go.
It's rather sad really, but there it is."*

Work Face

Bored

Top Five

Best songs for a
long commute:
1. _____
2. _____
3. _____
4. _____
5. _____

Breaktime Brain Teasers

Which actor, who died on April 5,
2008, was originally considered for
the role of Chief Brody in the 1975
film *Jaws*?

Answers from previous page

Mind Games

Boss says:
"I'm working on it."
Boss means:
"I'm completely
ignoring your request."

Unlikely Candidate

Glamour model

_____

Lunchtime Sudoku: Answer =

1	9	5	4	7	3	8	2	6
7	2	3	6	5	8	4	9	1
4	8	6	2	1	9	7	5	3
9	5	2	7	3	4	1	6	8
8	6	4	5	2	1	3	7	9
3	7	1	9	8	6	2	4	5
6	4	8	3	9	2	5	1	7
5	3	9	1	4	7	6	8	2
2	1	7	8	6	5	9	3	4

Get the Job:
Answer = Editor

Dice Man:
Answer = 5 - 3 + 1 x 2 = 6

Elastic Band Bowling

1. Make a fist-sized ball out of elastic bands, by winding them round one another.
2. Clear an alley down the center of the office.
3. Set up ten pins in the standard triangle (try paper cups, plastic bottles, or glue sticks).
4. You can now play ten pin bowling according to the usual rules. There is an additional skill in attempting to get the elastic band ball to roll in a straight line.
5. Rebounds from the wall behind the pins don't count.

Place Your Bets

Your new job will be:

Fulfilling, well-paid, glamorous —/—

Incomprehensible, odd, remote —/—

Dangerous, unstable, illegal —/—

The Bottom Line

GreedIsGood Corporation is projecting sales growth of 20% a year for the next five years. Their current turnover is $1 million. How big will their turnover be after two years if their targets are exactly achieved?

Thought for the Day

Work while it is called today, for you know not how much you will be hindered tomorrow. One today is worth two tomorrows; never leave that till tomorrow which you can do today.

Benjamin Franklin (1706-1790)

Answers from previous page

The One-Minute Zookeeper: Answer = One (One for each vowel in the animal's name)
Movie Quote: Answer = *Nanny McPhee* (2006)
Brain Teaser: Answer = Charlton Heston

Open Plan Hockey

Set up two goals at either end of a clear space (the legs of two chairs will do).

Use rulers or rolled up documents as hockey sticks.

Use a roll of sticky tape as the puck, you may find it slides across the floor better if it is wrapped in plastic or packing tape.

Two captains choose two teams. Hockey is best played in a kneeling position, with no contact allowed, though you may choose your own rules if you want a rougher version.

First team to five goals is the winner.

The losers buy post-match cakes for all.

Ways to Pass the Time

Arguing ☐

Consoling ☐

Shunning ☐

Design Your Own

Pie Chart:

Piggy Bank

You take your savings to the bank on a bicycle. On the way there you cycle at 16 miles per hour. On the way back you are tired and you cycle the exact same route at 12 miles per hour.

What was your average speed for the whole round trip?

Today's Greatest Achievement

Not speaking to anyone ☐

Not answering the phone ☐

Not crying in the bathroom ☐

In the Calendar

What happened on March 20, 1995?

Answers from previous page

The Bottom Line: Answer =$1.44 million

Watching Paint Dry

The decorators are in the office. On the wall you find the following series of letters painted, divided by curved lines.

V I B G Y O

What is the next letter?

Who Am I?

Can you work out which singer's name is hidden in the anagram below?

JAB ME SWORN

Work Face

New Office

Words to Impress Your Colleagues

Test yourself and expand your vocabulary.
Do you know the meaning of the word:

Nudiustertian?

My Next Meeting

Who _____

Where _____

Result _____

Today's Target

To write "You'll be lucky if it gets there" on all mail boxes

Brief Survival Guide

Employer Intrusion:

1. Garlic rub

3. Don't answer that phone

2. Keep stake handy

Mass Hysterias

Today we are all going to...
Start hoarding metal objects, sugar and cotton reels

Answers from previous page

Piggy Bank: Answer = 13.71 miles per hour (to 2 decimal places)

In the Calendar: Answer = Nerve gas attack on Tokyo subway

Office Sardines

This game is an excellent way to pass the time in a large office while maintaining an appearance of hard work. It can be played by two to ten players, depending on the size of the office.

All players gather in the meeting room, and pretend to have a meeting (you may want to have some spreadsheets and other documents to make it convincing).

One player leaves the room and finds a place to try to "hide." (This can be as simple as the stock room, a small corner office or the emergency stairwell).

The other players leave the meeting room to search for the hidden player—walking purposefully around the building holding documents until they find him. They can then pretend to continue their meeting as more players arrive in the crowded space, until the last player finds them. He or she is the loser and now has to hide in the next round of the game.

Ridiculous Rules

It is illegal not to tell the tax man anything you do not want him to know, but legal not to tell him information you do not mind him knowing.

Breaktime Brain Teasers

What breed of spaniel has been selected as Best in Show at Crufts more times than any other?

Clock Watching

Lunch is at 1:30 p.m. How much longer?

Work Space

The Andromeda Galaxy is our closest neighboring galaxy at 2.2 million light years away. It is so bright you can see it with your own eyes on a clear evening sky, away from city lights.

Answers from previous page

Watching Paint Dry: Answer = R (The first letters of the colors of the rainbow, reversed)

Who Am I? Answer = James Brown

Impress Your Colleagues: Answer = Nudiustertian refers to the day before yesterday.

Dice Man

A dice is thrown 20 times.

The total sum of the numbers thrown is 72.

By coincidence, each throw lands on a six or a three.

How many sixes were thrown?

Top Ten

Deli Fish Filling:

Salmon ☐
Trout ☐
Shark ☐
Octopus ☐
Cod ☐
Plaice ☐
Squid ☐
Halibut ☐
Swordfish ☐
Sturgeon ☐

Guess the Phobia

This occurs when you're nearing a deadline:

Chronophobia

The Bottom Line

The Fresh Air Corporation has $500,000 and pays half of this to be the sole provider of oxygen in the economy of Blunderland. It then charges $100 to each citizen and ends up with $600,000.

How many citizens live in Blunderland?

Morning Meditation

If a man who cannot count finds a four-leaf clover, is he lucky?

Stanislaw J. Lec

Clock Watching

How long is it until the 8:00 a.m. alarm call?

Answers from previous page

Clock Watching: Answer = Answer: 1 hour and 45 minutes

Brain Teaser: Answer = Cocker Spaniel

Design Your Own

[image of empty box]

Meeting room

Unlikely Candidate

Nobel Prize for Peace
_____

Who Bought The Cheese?

Abby, Barney and Carol go out shopping together.
They buy cheese, bread and wine.
The cheese is the most expensive item.
Altogether, they spend $32.00.
The bread costs $1.00 less than the wine and
$2.00 less than the cheese.
Carol and Barney pay for one item each, and
both pay with $2 dollar notes, receiving no change.
Abby spent less money than Barney.

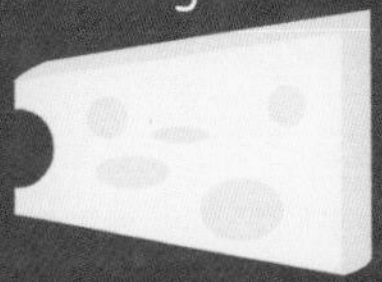

Who bought the cheese?

Whatever You Do

Don't even think about any of the following:

Badly scratched records playing over and over

Cold sores that won't heal

Screeching car tyres circling the building

Get the Job

Unscramble the anagram below to find the job.

Anagram Beg

Answer _____

Before They Were Famous

He is known for his role as Führer in Nazi Germany but what did Adolf Hitler do before he ruled the country?

Answer _____

Extinct Jobs

Dog Whipper:
A "dog whipper" worked in a church from the 16th to 19th centuries and had the job of removing badly behaved dogs from the church yard or service. Dogs often accompanied their owners to church and would be removed by the "dog whipper" and tied up until their owners collected them.

Answers from previous page

Guess the Phobia: Answer = Fear of time.
Clock Watching: Answer = 4 hours and 15 minutes
The Bottom Line: Answer = 3500
Dice Man: Answer = 4

Payday for Pessimists

It's finally the end of the week, but it's too cold to go out to celebrate.

Around the Water Cooler

- There's been a take-over bid
- There'll be no more pay rises
- There's talk of war

Domino Logic

Can you work out the missing number and the reason why?

= 7

= 16

= 7

= ?

Change the Word

In six steps...

Bore

_____

_____

_____

_____

_____

Dine

Today's Target

To put a huge pot plant in your boss's office while they are away from their desk.

Clock Watching

The server is off until 2:10 p.m. How long do you have to wait?

👁 Caught by the Boss

Hand in the till ☐

Hiding a bottle of vodka ☐

Flirting with his wife ☐

Answers from previous page

Who bought the cheese? Answer = Barney bought the cheese.

Get the Job: Answer = Garbage man

Before They Were Famous: Adolf Hitler painted picture postcards.

WORDWHEEL

Using only the letters in the Wordwheel, you have ten minutes to find as many words as possible, none of which may be plurals, foreign words or proper nouns. Each word must be of three letters or more, all must contain the central letter and letters can only be used once in every word.

There is at least one nine-letter word in the wheel.

Nine-letter word _____

The Bottom Line

The Happiness Foundation is charging $300 for a week-long retreat. They have three yurts in the woods and each yurt can take four guests.

How much revenue would they make if the retreats are fully booked for a year?

Excuses for...	Today's Target
Alcohol lunch: _____ _____	To say "I'll think about it" every time someone asks you any question.

Thought For the Day

There are really not many jobs that actually require a penis or a vagina, and all other occupations should be open to everyone.
   Gloria Steinem (American Writer and Activist)

Answers from previous page

Domino Logic: Answer = 10—Add together the total spots on the first and third dominos and subtract the total spots on the second domino right hand side, then add the results together.

Clock Watching: Answer = 4 hours and 25 minutes

Change the Word:
Bore, Bare, Care, Cane, Wane, Wine, Dine

Dice Man

Using three of the arithmetical signs +, -, x and ÷, can you achieve the correct total?

Payday for Pessimists

They've given you a pay rise... but cut your hours.

File Pile Hurdles

1. Collect all the pending files from people's in-trays around the office
2. Clear a "running track" around the desks and pile up the files. They can be piled as high as you want to jump.
3. Competitors then run the race, jumping over the piles of files. The winner is first to the finish line.

Lunchtime Sudoku

		8				9	4	1
2	3				1		7	
5				8	7			
3		5	2	6		1		
8			3		4			9
		7		1	5	2		4
			1	2				5
	7		9				6	3
9	5	6				8		

Get the Job

Can you unscramble the anagram below to get the job title?

Larios

Answer _____

Pick 'n' Mix

Choose 3 words to create the perfect meal:

Tomatoes Cheese

Carrots Potatoes

Chicken Garlic

Beef Mushrooms

Bread Butter

Answers from previous page

Wordwheel nine-letter word = Pointless
The Bottom Line: Answer = $187,200

Top Ten

Interview Shirt:

- Silk ☐
- Nylon ☐
- Cashmere ☐
- Velvet ☐
- Denim ☐
- Cotton ☐
- Wool ☐
- Acrylic ☐
- Chiffon ☐
- Muslin ☐

Board Meeting Doodle

Place Your Bets

The last sandwich left will be:

Tasty chicken salad — / —

Dried up sausage and onion — / —

An inedible rubbery mystery — / —

Named and Shamed

Not funny _____

Not clever _____

Not all there _____

Dice Man

A dice is thrown 10 times.
The total sum of the numbers
thrown is 36. By coincidence,
each throw lands on a three or
a four.
How many threes were thrown?

Whatever You Do

Don't even think about
any of the following:

Blisters on your feet

The thing that lives in the wardrobe

Soggy newspaper on the floor

Answers from previous page

Lunchtime Sudoku:

Get the Job:

Answer = Sailor

Dice Man:

Answer = 4 x 1 ÷ 4 + 5 = 6

7	6	8	5	3	2	9	4	1
2	3	4	6	9	1	5	7	8
5	1	9	4	8	7	3	2	6
3	4	5	2	6	9	1	8	7
8	2	1	3	7	4	6	5	9
6	9	7	8	1	5	2	3	4
4	8	3	1	2	6	7	9	5
1	7	2	9	5	8	4	6	3
9	5	6	7	4	3	8	1	2

Ways to Pass the Time

Arguing ☐

Miming ☐

Tinkering ☐

Design Your Own

Company pen

Office High Jump

All this game needs is a peice of string that can be tied between two desks, filing cabinets, photcopiers or bookcases.

Competitors begin by initially jumping over the string at a low hight that is gradually raised.

If someone makes contact with the string they are out of the competition.
The winner is the last person still in the game.

Brain Teaser

Which subatomic particle is named after the Greek for "first"?

Answer _____

Piggy Bank

A newspaper seller stocks the Daily Drivel and the Pomp City Times.
The Drivel costs $0.40, the Times costs $0.80.
On Monday he makes $66 from selling 100 newspapers.
On Tuesday he makes $70 from selling 100 newspapers to the same 100 customers.
How many customers switched from the Drivel to the Times?

Two-Word Horoscopes

Aries - Now now

Taurus - Stop it

Gemini - Cherry tart

Cancer - Did you?

Leo - Goodness hides

Virgo - Look sharp!

Libra - It's over

Scorpio - Last time

Sagittarius - Cool dude!

Capricorn - Darker ways

Aquarius - Oh, but...

Pisces - Try again

Answers from previous page

Dice Man: Answer = Four threes were thrown

Who Am I?

Which singer's name is hidden in the anagram below?

Triangle of Sea

Work Face

Hectic Weekend

Watching paint Dry

The decorators are in the office.

On the wall you find the following series of letters painted.

M T W T F S

What is the next letter?

Words to impress your colleagues

Test yourself and expand your vocabulary.
Do you know the meaning of the word:

Pulveratricious?

Sing While You Work

These lyrics are from a song about work.
Can you guess the song?

*"They say low wages are a reality
If we want to compete abroad."*

Today's Target

To close all doors behind you and tap on each three times afterward.

Brief Survival Guide

Overworked:

Answer "yes" to everything

Appear lost and confused

Pretend to be deaf

Mass Hysterias

Today we are all going to:
Inspect every item of food for images of the saints.

Answers to previous page

Brain Teaser: Answer = Proton

Piggy Bank: Answer = 10

Coffee Machine Sprinting

Create a starting line anywhere in your office and get someone to give the starting signal.

Each player must line up along the starting line and at the signal must race to the coffee machine

The first to the coffee machine gets 10 points.

Players must then make the coffees and when all coffees are made they must race back to the start line.

The winner is the one who crosses the start line first.

Work Space

The average temperature on Pluto is -390 degrees Fahrenheit.

Around the Water Cooler

It's never going to happen ▮

It is going to happen in the future ▮

It happened last night ▮

Ridiculous Rules

In London, Freemen are allowed to take a flock of sheep across London Bridge without being charged a toll; they are also allowed to drive geese down Cheapside.

In the Calendar

When was the first session of the U.S. Supreme Court in New York?

Top Five

Best songs for arguing with the boss:

1. _____
2. _____
3. _____
4. _____
5. _____

Answers from previous page

Watching Paint Dry: Answer = S (The first letters of the days of the week)

Who Am I? Answer = Gloria Estefan

Words: Pulveratricious means covered with dust

Sing While You Work: Answer = *Workingman's Blues #2* - Bob Dylan

Wordwheel

Using only the letters in the Wordwheel, you have ten minutes to find as many words as possible, none of which may be plurals, foreign words or proper nouns. Each word must be of three letters or more, all must contain the central letter and letters can only be used once in every word. There is at least one nine-letter word in the wheel.

Nine-letter word: _____

Guess the Phobia

What you get when your boss breezes past your desk all smiles and demands a meeting:

Ideophobia

Clock Watching

The meeting finishes at 11:30 a.m. How much longer?

Morning Meditation

A man with one watch knows what time it is; a man with two watches is never quite sure

Lee Segall

The Bottom Line

Cindy Little is knitting rainbow-colored waistcoats for poodles. It takes $50 worth of wool to make seven waistcoats, which sell for $10 each. In January she spent $600 on wool and sold all but four of the waistcoats.
How many did she sell?

Answers from previous page

In the Calendar: Answer = First session of the U.S. Supreme Court in New York was on February 1, 1790

Dice Man

A dice is thrown 30 times.
The total sum of the numbers thrown is 135.
By coincidence, each throw lands on a five or a two.

How many twos were thrown?

Design Your Own

Office carpet

Morning Meditation

Beware lest you lose the substance by grasping at the shadow

Aesop

Change the Word

In 6 steps:

Fine

_____

_____

_____

_____

Best

Place Your Bets

Your new office outfit defines you as:

Cool, trendy and happening —/—

Calm, clean and meticulous —/—

Confused and out of touch —/—

Named and Shamed

Nose job _____

Boob job _____

Facelift _____

Unlikely Candidate

Military Commander _____

Mass Hysterias

Today we are all going to:

Gibber like baboons and scratch our heads.

In the Calendar

When did the famous escapologist Houdini die?

Answers from previous page

The Bottom Line: Answer = 80

Clock Watching: Answer = 2 hours and 40 minutes

Guess the Phobia: Answer = Fear of ideas

Wordwheel nine-letter word = Assistant

The One-Minute Comedian

Here is a corny joke with the vowels (and "y"s and punctuation) removed and the letters put into groups of three.

MNW LKS NTB RCH

Can you decipher it?

Work Face

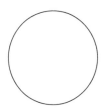

Huge Bonus

Unlikely Candidate

Groundbreaking Scientist

_____

Whatever you do...

Don't even think about any of the following:

Smelly socks

Smelly drains

Smelly cheese

Get the Job

Unscramble the anagram below to find the job.

Cannot Tuca

Answer _____

Before They Were Famous

Movie star Tom Cruise is now very open about his religious beliefs but before he became a star, he began training for a different career.
What was it?

Answer _____

Extinct Jobs

Tosher:
In London, during Victorian times, a "tosher" was someone who scavenged in sewers for items such as lost jewelry and coins. When they found a useful item they would clean it up and then sell it.

Answers from previous page:

Change the Word: Fine, Line, Lint, Lent, Went, West, Best

Dice Man: Answer = 5

In the Calendar: Answer = Houdini died on October 31, 1926

Domino Logic

What is the missing number?

=22

=23

=28

= ?

Breaktime Brain Teasers

What was lost by King John, melted down by Oliver Cromwell and almost stolen by Thomas Blood?

Answer _____

Which Movie Contains the Following Quote?

"Yeah, but your scientists were so preoccupied with whether or not they could, they didn't stop to think if they should."

Change the Word

Change Fake to Romp in 6 steps

Fake

_____

_____

_____

_____

_____

Romp

Sing While You Work

These are lyrics from a song about work. Can you name the song?

But when I get home to you
I find the things that you do
Will make me feel alright

Answers from previous page

Get the Job: Answer = Accountant

Before They Were Famous: Answer = Tom Cruise entered a seminary to become a priest.

The One-Minute Comedian: Answer = A man walks into a bar. Ouch!

Today's Target

To stare at someone without blinking for at least 3 minutes.

Wordwheel

Using only the letters in the wordwheel, you have ten minutes to find as many words as possible, none of which may be plurals, foreign words or proper nouns. Each word must be of three letters or more, all must contain the central letter and letters can only be used once in every word.

There is at least one nine-letter word in the wheel.

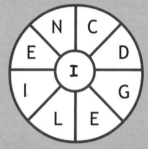

Nine-letter word _____

The Bottom Line

The Magic Dollar Press prints 50 fake $50 notes a week. The notes are sold in Jake's Bar for 20% of their face value. Jake is paid 5% of the revenue to not notice what is going on.

How long does it take Jake to earn a real $50?

Thought for the Day

Work is the refuge of people who have nothing better to do.

Oscar Wilde

Answers from previous page

Sing While You Work: Answer = *A Hard Day's Night* - The Beatles

Brain Teaser: Answer = The Crown Jewels

Change the Word: Fake, Fame, Dame, Damp, Lamp, Ramp, Romp

Dominoes: Answer = 24
(Multiply the right hand side by the left hand side on each domino, then add the totals together)

Movie Quote: *Jurassic Park* (1997)

Under Desk Leg Wrestling

Two people must sit opposite each other at a desk.

This works best if they are both sitting on wheeled office chairs.

Each chair must be at a certain distance from the desk. This distance must be equal.

The two competitors lock legs under the desk and pull.

The winner is the one who pulls the other's chair closest to the desk.

Dice Man

Using three of the arithmetical signs $+$, $-$, X and $\div$, can you achieve the correct total?

Payday for Pessimists

You won office bingo but now everyone expects a present.

Lunchtime Sudoku

		8				9	4	1
2	3				1		7	
5				8	7			
3		5	2	6		1		
8			3		4			9
		7		1	5	2		4
			1	2				5
	7		9				6	3
9	5	6				8		

Get the Job

Can you unscramble the anagram to reveal the job title?

Arrive Innate

Answer _____

Pick 'n' Mix

Choose 3 words to describe the current management:

Sensible	Useless
Senseless	Brutal
Considerate	Lazy
Cold-hearted	Liars
Trustworthy	
Untrustworthy	

Answers from previous page

The Bottom Line: Answer = Two weeks

Wordwheel nine-letter word: Diligence

The One-Minute Businessman

Here is a business catchphrase with the vowels (and 'y's and punctuation) removed and the letters put into groups of three. Can you decipher it?

THN KNG TSD THB X

Today's Greatest Achievement

Being helpful ▢

Matching socks ▢

Listening to colleagues ▢

Which Movie Contains the Following Quote?

"Human beings were not meant to sit in little cubicles staring at computer screens all day, filling out useless forms and listening to eight different bosses drone on about about mission statements."

Work Face

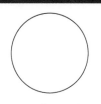

Confused

Top Five

Best songs for panicking like an idiot:

1. _____
2. _____
3. _____
4. _____
5. _____

Breaktime Brain Teasers

Which planet in the solar system is named after the Roman messenger to the Gods?

Answers from previous page

Mind Games

Boss says: "There was a slight communication failure."

Boss means: "I forgot to tell you."

Unlikely Candidate

Game show host

_____

Lunchtime Sudoku: Answer =

7	6	8	5	3	2	9	4	1
2	3	4	6	9	1	5	7	8
5	1	9	4	8	7	3	2	6
3	4	5	2	6	9	1	8	7
8	2	1	3	7	4	6	5	9
6	9	7	8	1	5	2	3	4
4	8	3	1	2	6	7	9	5
1	7	2	9	5	8	4	6	3
9	5	6	7	4	3	8	1	2

Get the Job:
Answer = Veterinarian

Dice Man:
Answer = 2 x 2 + 2 ÷ 2 = 3

Wheely Chair Cycling

For this event all you need are office chairs with wheels on them.

1. Competitors must sit on their chairs backward, (Facing the back of the chair).

2. Decide on a track around the office, moving desks if necessary.

3. The players must then pedal their chairs using their feet on the floor around the track.

4. The winner is the cyclist who crosses the finish line first.

Place Your Bets

The roads this morning will be:

Empty, fast and easy	—/—
Stagnant, hopeless and upsetting	—/—
Full of colorful people and their lovely cars	—/—

Word Mania

Can you see the one three-letter word which can be added on to these starting letter to make new words?:

SH - - -

CR - - -

DR - - -

AL - - -

CL - - -

Thought for the Day

If A equals success, then the formula is A equals X plus Y and Z, with X being work, Y play, and Z keeping your mouth shut.

Albert Einstein

Answers from previous page

The One-Minute Businessman: Answer = Thinking outside the box

Movie Quote: Answer = *Office Space* (1999)

Brain Teaser: Answer = Mercury

Paper Airplane Race

Make a paper airplane following the diagrams above.
You could use a recent staff appraisal, written warning or offensive email.
Create a line on the office floor.
Each player must throw their airplane toward the line.
The winner is the person whose airplane flies furthest over the line.

Ways to Pass the Time

Bossing ☐

Busying ☐

Blathering ☐

Design Your Own

Paperweight:

Piggy Bank

In the piggy bank there are only $2 bills and $5 dollar bills. To count them, you divide the $5 bills into eight equal piles, and the $2 bills into nine equal piles.
One of the piles of $5 bills contains thirty dollars. The total amount in the piggy bank is $294.
How many $2 bills are there in each of the nine piles?

Today's Greatest Achievement

Seat on the bus/train ▮

Extra half an hour in bed ▮

Free drinks ▮

In the Calendar

In what year was the Battle of Waterloo marking the end of the Napoleonic empire?

Answers from previous page

Word Mania: Answer = One

Watching Paint Dry

The decorators are spring-cleaning the office.

On the wall you find the following series of letters painted.

A M J J A S O

What is the next letter?

Who Am I?

Can you work out which actor's name is hidden in the anagram below?

DICTATE SLOW NO

Work Face

Bankrupt

Words to Impress Your Colleagues

Test yourself and expand your vocabulary.

Do you know the meaning of the word:

Rastaquouere

My Next Job

When	_____
About	_____
Meaning	_____

Today's Target

To ask those around you not to speak to you until noon.

Brief Survival Guide

Business Lunch:

1. Alcohol
2. Loose-fitting pants
3. Afternoon nap

Mass Hysterias

Today we are all going to...
Strap ourselves to the nearest desk in case of flooding.

Answers from previous page

Piggy Bank: Answer = Three
In the Calendar: Answer = The Battle of Waterloo was in 1815.

Wheely Tug of War

Clear a space in the office.

Draw a winning line in the middle of the cleared space.

The contestants divide into teams of one to five per team.

Each team takes hold of one end of the same piece of rope as in a normal tug of war.

The players sit on office chairs and may not stand up during the contest. If any players stand or fall off their chairs, they are disqualified.

Once the contest starts, each team must try to pull the opposing team toward the winning line. Once the lead player in the opposing team is pulled over the line, the contest is won.

Ridiculous Rules

In Bahrain, a male doctor may legally examine a woman's genitals but is forbidden from looking directly at them during the examination; he may only see their reflection in a mirror.

Breaktime Brain Teasers

Which U.S. president said this? "Its soul, its climate, its equality, liberty, laws, people, and manners. My god! how little do my countrymen know what precious blessings they are in possession of, and which no other people on earth enjoy!"

Clock Watching

Coffee break is at 10:45 a.m. How much longer?

Work Space

If the planet Jupiter was hollow, you could fit about 1,400 Earth-sized planets inside of it with a little room to spare.

Answers from previous page

Watching Paint Dry: Answer = N (The first letters of the months of the year, starting in April)

Who Am I? Answer = Clint Eastwood

Impress Your Colleagues: Answer = A Rastaquouere is a social upstart

Dice Man

A dice is thrown 50 times.

The total sum of the numbers thrown is 85.

By coincidence, each throw lands on a one or a two.

How many ones were thrown?

Top Ten

Desktop Fruitbowl:

Apples ☐
Oranges ☐
Bananas ☐
Pineapple ☐
Pears ☐
Strawberries ☐
Blueberries ☐
Raspberries ☐
Plums ☐
Cherries ☐

Guess the Phobia

This may happen if you accidentally overhear gossip about yourself:

Onomatophobia

Morning Meditation

The obscure we see eventually.
The completely obvious, it seems, takes longer.

Edward R. Murrow

In the Calendar

In what year and where did Napoleon Bonaparte die?

The Bottom Line

In 2001 WowOMG.Com borrowed $1,000,000 to fund "an undertaking of great advantage, but nobody can know what it is." Their total costs before the inevitable bankruptcy were $1,000,000.05 Their total revenues were $1.23. How much money did they manage to lose?

Answers from previous page

Clock watching: Answer = 2 hours and 50 minutes

Brain Teaser: Answer = Thomas Jefferson

Design Your Own

Wacky pencil

Unlikely Candidate

Sober _____

Where Is My Cheese?

▲ ■ ●

Picture these moves in your head, and keep careful track.
Swap the square with the circle.
Swap the green shape with the red shape.
Put the cheese inside the middle box.
Swap the square with the circle.
Swap the green shape with the red shape.
Move the cheese to the box on the left hand end.
Swap the square with the circle.
Swap the green shape with the red shape.
Is the cheese on the left, on the right, or in the middle?

Whatever You Do

Don't even think about:
Outer space and alien invasions
How far away you are from home
Grinding gears on a twenty-year-old car

Get the Job

Unscramble the anagram below to find the job.

Dreg Earn

Answer _____

Before They Were Famous

We know him as a Hollywood tough guy but what job did Sylvester Stallone do before he was famous?

Answer _____

Extinct Jobs

Mudlark:
"Mudlarks" were people who, in 19th century England, dredged the banks of the River Thames in early morning when the tide was out. They waded through unprocessed sewage, and sometimes dead bodies, to find little treasures to sell.

Answers from previous page

In the Calendar: Answer = May 5, 1821 on the island of St. Helena
Guess the Phobia: Answer = Fear of hearing a certain word or name.
The Bottom Line: Answer = $999,998.82
Dice Man: Answer = 15

Payday for Pessimists

This payday you've been invited out with colleagues but you're not going because you don't like them.

Sing While You Work...

Which song about work do the lyrics below come from?

Friday night's pay night guys fresh out of work,
Talking about the weekend scrubbing off the dirt.

Domino Logic

Can you work out the missing number and the reason why?

= 10

= 2

= 8

= ?

Change the Word

In six steps...

Hall
___
___
___
___
___
Paid

Today's Target

To re-arrange the coffee area during a board meeting

Clock Watching

The late shift ends at 1:00 a.m. How long until then?

Caught by the Boss

Speaking badly of his wife ☐

Speaking badly of his car ☐

Speaking badly of his haircut ☐

Answers from previous page

Where is My Cheese? Answer =
In the middle, in the blue square.

Get the Job: Answer = Gardener

Before They Were Famous: Sylvester Stallone cleaned out lions' cages.

WORDWHEEL

Using only the letters in the Wordwheel, you have ten minutes to find as many words as possible, none of which may be plurals, foreign words or proper nouns. Each word must be of three letters or more, all must contain the central letter and letters can only be used once in every word.
There is at least one nine-letter word in the wheel.

Nine-letter word _____

The Bottom Line

Last year Splendid Sofas had $100,000 of debt and $2,000,000 turnover of which 10% is profit. They were paying 5% a year on the debt. This year they have the same debt, but the interest rate doubles, while their turnover halves, but profit as a percentage of the turnover doubles.

What percentage of their profit this year goes toward paying the debt?

Thought For the Day

Three Rules of Work: Out of clutter find simplicity; from discord find harmony; In the middle of difficulty lies opportunity.
Albert Einstein

Answers from previous page

Domino Logic: Answer = : 6
(Add together the total spots on the second and third dominos, then subtract the total spots on the first)
Clock Watching: Answer = 4 hours and 20 minutes
Change the Word:
Hall, Haul, Maul, Mail, Main, Pain, Paid
Sing While You Work: Answer = *Working in the Highway* Bruce Springsteen

Dice Man

Using three of the arithmetical signs
+, -, × and ÷,
can you achieve the correct total?

Payday for Pessimists

Another month gone by and you're
still saving for that vacation.

File Pile Hopscotch

1. Make a layout on the floor from all
your in-tray files
2. Each file should be given a
numerical value.
3. Competitors then throw an eraser
onto the files and note where it lands
and what the value is. They must then
hop over the files. They must not
touch the file where the eraser landed.
4. The winner is the one who finishes
with the most points.

Lunchtime Sudoku

	5				8	7	6	
6	4	8						9
			2	3	4			
5			4	3		1		2
	9	1		7	8			
4		7		6	2			3
		4	5	9				
9						3	1	8
		7	2	3			5	

Get the Job

Can you unscramble
the anagram below
to get the job title?

Shine Farm

Answer _____

Pick 'n' Mix

Choose 3 words to
describe a perfect
vacation destination:

Sunny	Sea
Snowy	Rivera
Wilderness	Mountains
Cottage	Activity
Hotel	Beach

Answers from previous page

Wordwheel nine-letter word = Corporate
The Bottom Line: Answer = 5%

Top Ten

Desktop Photographs

Baby ☐
Mother ☐
Father ☐
Sister ☐
Brother ☐
Friends ☐
You ☐
Wife ☐
Husband ☐
Pets ☐

Board Meeting Doodle

The Filing Cabinet

Which is the odd word out?

BEE-EATER
JOSS-STICK
TOLL-BOOTH
CROSS-SECTION
EGG-GLASS
PUFF-FISH
BELL-LIKE

Whatever You Do

Don't even think about
any of the following:

Splinters in your fingernails

Fairground rides that spin you round

Sunburn on your sensitive bits

Answers from previous page

Place Your Bets

Your nice surprise today is:

A lucrative unexpected bonus —/—

A pay raise and promotion —/—

You're fired —/—

Named and Shamed

Lecherous leech _____

Neurotic catastrophy _____

Senseless _____

Lunchtime Sudoku:

2	5	3	9	4	8	7	6	1
6	4	8	7	1	5	2	3	9
7	9	1	6	2	3	4	8	5
5	8	6	4	3	9	1	7	2
3	2	9	1	5	7	8	4	6
4	1	7	8	6	2	5	9	3
8	3	4	5	9	1	6	2	7
9	6	5	2	7	4	3	1	8
1	7	2	3	8	6	9	5	4

Get the Job:

Answer = Fisherman

Dice Man:

Answer = 4 ÷ 2 + 1 x 2 = 6

Ways to Pass the Time

Reading ☐

Rocking ☐

Reprimanding ☐

Design Your Own

Panic room

Office Chair Slalom

Organize a course through desks and filing cabinets.

The course should resemble a slalom race weaving around the office furniture.

Each player must sit on their chairs facing the back and manoevre the chair along the floor using their feet.
As each player attempts the course they should be timed.

The winner is the player who completes the course cleanly in the fastest time.

Brain Teaser

In which year did the artist Pablo Picasso die?

Answer _____

Piggy Bank

My first is in More, but not in Less.

My second is in Profit, but not in Perfect.

My third is in Union but not in Chorus.

My fourth is in Desk, but not in Draws.

My fifth is in Sorry but not in Sound.

I make the world go round. What am I?

Two-Word Horoscopes

Aries - Lazy days

Taurus - What's there?

Gemini - Broader sights

Cancer - Little glories

Leo - Big news

Virgo - Terrible vision

Libra - Grow some

Scorpio - Pitiful offerings

Sagittarius - No warning

Capricorn - Top times

Aquarius - No, no

Pisces - Stay home

Answers from previous page

The Filing Cabinet: Answer = Toll-booth
(the other hyphenated words contain the same letter three times in a row)

Who Am I?

Which singer's name is hidden in the anagram below?

Built-in maker jest.

Work Face

Major Crisis

The Filing Cabinet

What do these words have in common?

ACCEPT   DEFLUX

BEGINS   FLOORS

CHIMPS   KNOTTY

CHOOSY

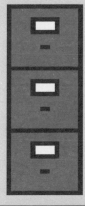

Words to Impress Your Colleagues

Test yourself and expand your vocabulary

Do you know the meaning of the word:

Inaniloquent?

Sing While You Work

These lyrics are from a song about work. Can you guess the song?

Eight or ten hours a day of work and toil and sweat
Always got somebody lookin' down his neck.

Today's Target

Have a long conversation with a random stranger about house pests.

Brief Survival Guide

Targets Meeting:

Confusing calculations

Scratch your head a lot

Fiddle with your shoes

Mass Hysterias

Today we are all going to:
Invest our life savings in tulips

Answers to previous page

Brain Teaser: Answer = 1973

Piggy Bank: Answer = Money

Expenses Conundrum

You get home after a night of business entertaining and realize you have taken home three receipts. One is yours, but the other two were left on the table by strangers who left before you.

You can remember that you paid for eight pina coladas and three lemonades, that pina coladas cost four times as much as lemonade, and that you added exactly 20% to the bill.

The receipts are not itemized—they are for $72.00, $84.00 and $103.00. Which one is your receipt and should you claim for one, two or three of the receipts?

Work Space

To reach outer space, you need to travel at least 50 miles from the Earth's surface.

Around the Water Cooler

He's missed the point ⬛

They've all gone crazy ⬛

We must be out of our minds ⬛

Ridiculous Rules

In Boulder, Colorado, it is illegal to kill a bird inside the city limits. It is also illegal to "own" a pet so inhabitants who keep animals are called "pet minders."

In the Calendar

What happened on September 1, 1939?

Top Five

Best songs for having a quiet cry:
1. _____
2. _____
3. _____
4. _____
5. _____

Wordwheel

Using only the letters in the Wordwheel, you have ten minutes to find as many words as possible, none of which may be plurals, foreign words or proper nouns. Each word must be of three letters or more, all must contain the central letter and letters can only be used once in every word. There is at least one nine-letter word in the wheel.

Nine-letter word: _____

Guess the Phobia

The person who suffers from this thinks of themselves as important:

Nomophobia

The Bottom Line

Hoopla TV pay $145,000 for the rights to show the Superbowl highlights on their cable feed. The pay-per-view fee is $10 if you book seven days in advance, or $15 if you book in the last week. Three quarters of the customers book at the $10 rate and the remainder pay $15. Hoopla lose $10,000 on the deal.
How many customers were there altogether?

Clock Watching

The afternoon break is at 3:00 p.m. How long do you have to wait?

Morning Meditation

Losing an illusion makes you wiser than finding a truth

Ludwig Börne

Answers from previous page

In the Calendar: Answer = Germany invaded Poland
Expenses conundrum: Answer = $84. And we won't tell if you don't tell.

Dice Man

Using three of the arithmetical signs +, −, X and ÷ , can you achieve the correct total?

[die: 2] [die: 3] [die: 3] [die: 3] = [die: 6]

Morning Meditation

You never know what is enough, until you know what is more than enough.

William Blake, (*Proverbs of Hell*)

Design Your Own

Personalized diary:

Guess the Real Word

Amphigory	☐
Absocelleny	☐
Absodoculane	☐

Change the Word

In 6 steps:

Scarf

_____

_____

_____

_____

_____

Phone

Place Your Bets

Today, _____ will eat:

Two dozen donuts	—/—
A pizza sandwich with fries	—/—
Everything in sight, offered or not	—/—

Named and Shamed

Compulsive shopper	_____
Meanest money grabber	_____
Big spender	_____

Unlikely Candidate

Media mogul _____

Mass Hysterias

Today we are all going to:

Throw a colleague into the river to see if they float.

In the Calendar

When was the first public reading of the Declaration of Independence?

Answers from previous page

The Bottom Line: Answer = 12,000
Clock Watching: Answer = Only 50 minutes
Guess the Phobia: Answer = fear of being out of cell phone contact
Wordwheel nine-letter word = Monitored

Expenses Conundrum

Following a long business trip around major cities, you realize you've lost all your receipts and tickets. You have to guess at the expense of each flight and come up with the following tally:

MUMBAI $330
BERLIN $420
CHICAGO $430
MELBOURNE $540
LOS ANGELES $640
PARIS $320

Can you work out what price you claimed for the London flight?

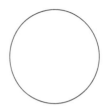

Work Face

Disciplinary Action

Unlikely Candidate

Oscar-winning actor
_____

Whatever You Do

Don't even think about any of the following:

Anything described as "cute"

"I-ay-ay will always love yooooou"

Vomiting after an evening out

Get the Job

Unscramble the anagram below to find the job.

Topmost Tier

Answer _____

Before They Were Famous

Jennifer Lopez has acted and sung her way to Hollywood stardom. Do you know what her job was before she hit the big time?

Answer _____

Extinct Jobs

Gong Farmer:
A "gong farmer" removed human excrement from privies and cesspits during the Tudor era in England. "Gong" was another word for dung. They worked at night and the waste they collected, called "night soil," was taken outside the city boundaries. Due to the excrement's noxious fumes, they often died of asphyxiation.

Answers from previous page:

Change the Word: Scarf, Scare, Score, Store, Stone, Shone, Phone
Dice Man: Answer = Answer: $3 \div 3 \times 3 + 3 = 6$
In the Calendar: Answer = July 8, 1776
Guess the Real Word: Answer = Amphigory (A nonsense verse.)

Domino Logic

What is the missing number?

=4

=5

=6

= ?

Payday for Pessimists

You've been paid but it doesn't even make a dent in your credit card bills.

Breaktime Brain Teasers

Which President said these words? "Whenever I hear any one arguing for slavery I feel a strong impulse to see it tried on him personally."

Answer _____

Which Movie Contains the Following Quote?

"You can bend the rules plenty once you get to the top, but not while you're trying to get there. And if you're someone like me, you can't get there without bending the rules."

Today's Target

To ask "Why?" every time someone asks you to do anything, or asks you for anything.

Change the Word

Change Bump to Type in 6 steps

Bump

_____

_____

_____

_____

_____

Type

Sing While You Work

These are lyrics from a song about work. Can you name the song?

Nine a.m. on the hour hand and she's waiting for the bell.

Answers from previous page

Get the Job: Answer = Optometrist

Before They Were Famous: Answer = Jennifer Lopez was a legal assistant.

Expenses Conundrum: Answer = $420 - $100 per consonant in each place name, $10 per vowel

Wordwheel

Using only the letters in the wordwheel, you have ten minutes to find as many words as possible, none of which may be plurals, foreign words or proper nouns. Each word must be of three letters or more, all must contain the central letter and letters can only be used once in every word.

There is at least one nine-letter word in the wheel.

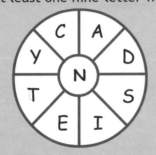

Nine-letter word _____

Excuses for...

Unplugging the phone:

_____

Work Face

Computer Virus

The Bottom Line

In the telesales department there are three men and three women working.

Alf sells $1,000 more Bert, and $2,000 more than Chris.
Annie sells twice as much as Alf.
Bronwen sells three times as much as Bert.
Cathy sells twice as much as Chris.

Total sales are $50,000
What was Cathy's sales total?

Thought for the Day

The future influences the present just as much as the past.

Friedrich Nietzsche

Answers from previous page

Sing While You Work: Answer = *She Works Hard for the Money* Donna Summer

Brain Teaser: Answer = Abraham Lincoln

Change the Word: Type, Tape, Tame, Lame, Lamp, Lump, Bump

Dominoes: Answer = Answer: 3 (Add together the total spots on the first domino and ignore the other dominoes)

Movie Quote: Answer = *Working Girl* (1988)

Trick Talk Champions

This game can help to make a long meeting or sales conference more exciting...

Agree a list of meaningless phrases that your colleagues or managers tend to use. Examples might include "blue sky thinking," "low-hanging fruit," or "thinking outside of the box."

Having agreed the list of phrases, each player may nominate one person in the meeting as their "champion". Use your skill and judgment to pick the participant who will use the most meaningless phrases.

During the meeting, keep one sheet of paper (preferably concealed beneath something that looks more important) with the list of phrases and a column for each champion. Every time they use one of the nominated phrases put a tick in the column, signifying one point.

At the end of the meeting, collate the results and see whose champion has been the winner. You may wish to agree a secret signal to be used for the first champion to reach five points—for instance placing both hands on top of your head, or turning your head to the left.

Dice Man

Using three of the arithmetical signs +, −, X and ÷, can you achieve the correct total?

Payday for Optimists

You've just invited a colleague for an after work drink and been turned down. Still, think of the money you've saved.

Get the Job

Can you unscramble the anagram to reveal the job title?

Brocade Star

Answer _____

Pick 'n' Mix

Choose 3 words to describe the perfect after-work cocktail:

Vodka   Lemon
Lime   Orange
Water   Rum
Whisky   Gin
Tequilla   Soda

Answers from previous page

The Bottom Line: Answer = $8,000

Wordwheel nine-letter word: Syndicate

The One-Minute Philosopher

Here is a philosophical quote with the vowels (and "y's" and punctuation) removed and the letters put into groups of three.
Can you decipher it?

THN XMN DLF SNT WRT HLV NG

Work Face

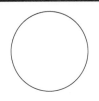

Overslept

Mind Games

Boss says: "I'll give you the basics, you can fill in the rest."

Boss means: "I can't be bothered with this."

Top Five

Best songs for clearing out your in-tray:

1. _____
2. _____
3. _____
4. _____
5. _____

Unlikely Candidate

Health Guru

_____

Today's Greatest Achievement

Hangover cure that works ☐
Hiding from boss all day ☐
Opening all your bills ☐

Which Movie Contains the Following Quote?

"Advertizing has us chasing cars and clothes, working jobs we hate so we can buy sh*t we don't need. . . . our Great Depression is our lives. We've all been raised on television to believe that one day we'd all be millionaires and movie gods and rock stars. But we won't. And we're slowly learning that fact."

Breaktime Brain Teasers

In what year was the Magna Carta (the origin of the modern concept of constitutional rule), signed by King John at Runnymede?

Answers from previous page

Get the Job: Answer = Broadcaster

Dice Man: Answer = 1 x 6 + 2 - 3 = 5

Wheely Chair Sumo Wrestling

For this event all you need are office chairs with wheels on them.

1. Two competitors must sit on their chairs backward, (facing the back of the chair), in opposite corners from each other.

2. At an agreed starting sound the two competitors must wheel toward each other and wrestle across the back of their chairs.

3. Each player must attempt to push their opponent off the wheely chair and onto the floor.

4. The winner is the wrestler who manages to get the most opponents onto the floor.

Place Your Bets

_____ 's first words today will be:

Where's my coffee?	—/—
Late again?	—/—
How lovely you could make it!	—/—

Word Mania

Can you see the one three-letter word which can be added on to these starting letters to make new words?:

SH - - -

WH - - -

M - - -

S - - -

REG - - -

Thought for the Day

Work while it is called today, for you know not how much you will be hindered tomorrow. One today is worth two tomorrow's; never leave that till tomorrow which you can do today.

Benjamin Franklin

Trick Talk Detector

Your boss calls an early morning meeting to "check that we have all our ducks in a row."

What is the real purpose of the meeting?

A: To force you to get to work on time for the first time this month.

B: To line up a series of toy ducks in an attempt to raise office morale.

C: To convince himself that his management role is not completely superfluous.

D: To torment you by using intentionally meaningless buzz phrases.

Answer: Who knows? Maybe you could call in sick?

Ways to pass the Time

Appropriating ☐

Accusing ☐

Asking ☐

Design Your Own

Work uniform:

Piggy Bank

On a private jet from New York to Frankfurt, a CEO putts a golf ball into a cup.
The plane travels 1.2 miles in the time it takes the ball to go from the club to the cup.
The jet is flying at 432 miles per hour.
The CEO's company is losing $120,000 a minute.
How much money did the company lose while the ball was on its way from the club to the cup?

Today's Greatest Achievement

New chocolate cookies ☐

Showering before dressing ☐

Finishing the sales reports ☐

In the Calendar

In what year was Communist China founded?

Answers from previous page

Word Mania: Answer = Ale

The Filing Cabinet

Which is the odd word out?

ABSTEMIOUS
COMMUNICATIVE
REACQUISITION
DISCOURAGES
ANTI-ABSOLUTIST
PARSIMONIOUSNESS
SEMI-AUTONOMOUS

Who Am I?

Can you work out
which singer's name is hidden
in the anagram below?

PARALYSES LOVE RAIN

Work Face

Voluntary redundancy

Words to Impress Your Colleagues

Test yourself and expand your vocabulary.

Do you know the meaning of the word:

Phenakism

My Next Review

Place _____

Type _____

Point? _____

Today's Target

To say "Yes!" but look doubtful every time some one asks you for anything.

Brief Survival Guide

Directors Meeting:
1. Alcohol
2. The onset of a sudden and very contagious illness
3. Get lost on your way to work

Mass Hysterias

Today we are all going to...
Build a boat and burn it at midnight!

Answers from previous page

Piggy Bank: Answer = $20,000, but it's OK, the CEO bet the captain $25,000 he could make the putt.

In the Calendar: Answer = 1949

Wordwheel

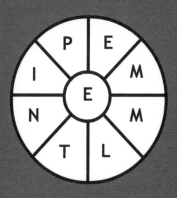

Using only the letters in the Wordwheel, you have ten minutes to find as many words as possible, none of which may be plurals, foreign words or proper nouns. Each word must be of three letters or more, all must contain the central letter and letters can only be used once in every word. There is at least one nine-letter word in the wheel.

Nine-letter word: _____

Ridiculous Rules

In Arizona, in the United States of America, you may be imprisoned for 25 years for cutting down a cactus. Also, in the same State, donkeys are apparently not permitted to sleep in bathtubs.

Breaktime Brain Teasers

Under which American President did the United States invade the Caribbean island of Grenada?

Answer _____

Clock Watching

How long is it until your 7:00 p.m. date?

Work Space

The average life span of a yellow star, like our Sun, is about 10 billion years. The Sun will eventually burn out in about 5 to 6 billion years.

Word Fits

Complete these words using three four-letter words. In each group of three, the missing word is the same.

T - - - -   S P - - - -   - - - - S T
W - - - - A S   T - - - - E R   C O L - - - -
S P - - - -   - - - - Y   - - - N T

Top Ten

Flip Chart Artwork:

Ink ☐
Oil paint ☐
Pencil ☐
Charcoal ☐
Crayon ☐
Watercolour ☐
Chalk ☐
Felt tip pen ☐
Acrylic paint ☐
Spray paint ☐

Guess the Phobia

This could occur when you're forced to do a mountain of photocopying:

Papyrophobia

Morning Meditation

You can't wake a person who is pretending to be asleep

Navajo Proverb

In the Calendar

When did the First World War start?

Paperclip Javelin

Clear a space in your office.
Each contestant fashions three minature javelins out of paperclips.
You can use up to five paperclips and twist or glue them together.
Take turns to throw the javelins from behind a line.
The javelin that hits the ground the furthest from the line is the winner.

Answers from previous page

Clock Watching: Answer = 8 hours and 10 minutes
Wordwheel nine-letter word = Implement
Brain Teaser: Answer = Ronald Regan

Design Your Own

[blank box]

Office Chair

Unlikely Candidate

Cosmetic Surgeon

_____

The Word Calculator

Find the alternative words that make this sum work:

TRICK

+ TYPE

_____

= RESTRICT

1	2	3	0	+
4	5	6	%	-
7	8	9	:	=

Whatever You Do

Don't even think about any of the following:

Greasy hair on your boss's head

Stubbly legs under the desk

Itchy wool against your neck

Get the Job

Unscramble the anagram below to find the job.

Rise Old

Answer _____

Before They Were Famous

We knew him as a highly regarded Hollywood movie star but what did Marlon Brando do before he was famous?

Extinct Jobs

Portager:

During the time of the Vikings a "portager" was someone who carried items aboard their ships and even sometimes the ships themselves. Both women and men were employed in this job.

Answers from previous page

In the Calendar: Answer = August 1, 1914

Guess the Phobia: Answer = Fear of paper

Word Fits: Answer = Here, Rain, Late

Payday for Optimists

You've got a bonus! You can try to work out how long it's going to take to get a 30ft yacht like your boss's.

Sing While You Work...

Which song about work do the lyrics below come from?

Damned if you do, damned if you don't I'm supposed to get a raise week, you know damn well I won't.

Domino Logic

Can you work out the missing number and the reason why?

🁲	🀹	🁜	= 34
🁣	🀹	🀺	= 45
🀽	🀻	🁜	= 27
🀸	🀿	🁗	= ?

Change the Word

In six steps...

Live

_____

_____

_____

_____

_____

Rant

Today's Target

Wear something blue and stroke it as if it is very special

Clock Watching

Lunch is at 3:20 p.m. How much longer?

👁 Caught by the Boss

Laughing at your boss's clothes ☐

Laughing at your colleagues socks ☐

Laughing when someone gets upset ☐

Answers from previous page

Word Calculator:
Answer = Con (Trick) + Strain (Type) = Constrain (Restrain)

Get the Job: Answer = Soldier

Before They Were Famous: Marlon Brando dug ditches

WORDWHEEL

Using only the letters in the Wordwheel, you have ten minutes to find as many words as possible, none of which may be plurals, foreign words or proper nouns. Each word must be of three letters or more, all must contain the central letter and letters can only be used once in every word.
There is at least one nine-letter word in the wheel.

Nine-letter word _____

The One-Minute Philosopher

Here is a philosophical quote with the vowels (and "y"s and punctuation) removed and the letters put into groups of three. Can you decipher it?

THN KTH RFR M

Thought For the Day

Coming together is a beginning.
Keeping together is progress.
Working together is success.
Henry Ford

Answers from previous page

Domino Logic: Answer = 51
(Multiply the total spots on the first domino by the total spots on the third, then subtract the total spots on the second domino.mino, then add the results together)

Clock Watching: Answer = 3 hours and 10 minutes

Change the Word:
Hear, Rear, Ream, Roam, Room, Boom

Sing While You Work: Answer = *Workin for a Livin*
Huey Lewis and the News

Dice Man

Using three of the arithmetical signs
+, -, x and ÷,

can you achieve the correct total?

Office Figure Skating

This game works in offices with smooth carpets or floors.

Remove your shoes and apply packing tape to the base of your feet.

Each contestant has three minutes to perform a freeform ice skating routine

The other contestants hold up their scores out of ten.

The contestant with the highest point score is the winner

(Note: This game should not be played without a formal health and safety assessment, which means it almost certainly won't be played. So basically, don't even think about it.)

Payday for Pessimists

You earn $100,000 per year but your overdraft remains the same.

Lunchtime Sudoku

	3		4	9		6	1	
					5	4	7	2
	8	2		1				9
			9	8				7
8		6				9		3
7				6	1			
1				2		5	3	
6	2	4	3					
	5	9		4	7		8	

Get the Job

Can you unscramble the anagram below to get the job title?

Chuff Urea

Answer _____

Pick 'n' Mix

Choose 3 words to describe the perfect day:

Holiday   Solitude

Sun   Alcoholic

Easy   Picnic

Busy   Lazy

Friends   Fun

Answers from previous page

Wordwheel nine-letter word = Visionary

The One-Minute Philosopher: Answer = *I think therefore I am* (Descartes)

Top Ten

Pets to Talk About:

Cat ☐
Dog ☐
Rabbit ☐
Hamster ☐
Mice ☐
Parrot ☐
Guinea pig ☐
Horse ☐
Fish ☐
Snake ☐

Board Meeting Doodle

The Filing Cabinet

Which is the odd word out?

EASE
IOTA
AUTO
AURA
OUZO
EACH
OOZE

Whatever You Do

Don't even think about
any of the following:

Frosted lipstick

Aniseed flavor alcohol

Used fly paper

Place Your Bets

Your boss phones you because:

You owe him money —/—

You want his job —/—

You're not at work —/—

Answers from previous page

Named and Shamed

Tyrant _____

Traitor _____

Tell tale _____

Lunchtime Sudoku:

Get the Job:

Answer = Chauffeur

Dice Man:

Answer = 5 - 3 ÷ 2 + 4 = 5

5	3	7	4	9	2	6	1	8
9	6	1	8	3	5	4	7	2
4	8	2	7	1	6	3	5	9
2	4	5	9	8	3	1	6	7
8	1	6	5	7	4	9	2	3
7	9	3	2	6	1	8	4	5
1	7	8	6	2	9	5	3	4
6	2	4	3	5	8	7	9	1
3	5	9	1	4	7	2	8	6

Ways to Pass the Time

Wandering ☐

Wilfully ☐

Wistfully ☐

Design Your Own

Funky laptop

Pass The Envelope

Put any document that you don't want to work on into an envelope

Plug in the computer speakers and play some music.

While the music is playing the envelope gets passed around the room.

The person who is holding the envelope when the music stops must sit out the next game.

Keep playing un til there is only one player left.

Brain Teaser

What was Muhammad Ali's birth name?

Answer _____

Piggy Bank

Tompkins, a customer in the fruit store, has the following preferences:

He likes banana more than peach.
He likes onion more than pear.
He likes potato more than spinach.

Will he like pear or asparagus better?

Two Word Horoscopes

Aries - Why me?

Taurus - Great emptiness

Gemini - Funny bones

Cancer - Little mistakes

Leo - Work it!

Virgo - Last gasps

Libra - Out there

Scorpio - Nosy neighbours

Sagittarius - Gossip monger

Capricorn - Last attempt

Aquarius - Best practice

Pisces - Beautiful outfit

Answers from previous page

The Filing Cabinet: Answer = Each
(the other words contain three vowels)

Who Am I?

Which president's name is hidden in the anagram below?

We're gush gob

Work Face

Office romance

The Filing Cabinet

Which is the odd word out?

DEFENCELESS

UNSCRUPULOUS

BANANAS

POW-WOW

SPILLING

RAZZMATAZZ

Words to Impress Your Colleagues

Test yourself and expand your vocabulary

Do you know the meaning of the word:

Finnimbrun?

Sing While You Work

These lyrics are from a song about work. Can you guess the song?

If you believe like workin' hard all day,
Just step in my shoes and take my pay.

Today's Target

Eat only food that is orange and drinks that are yellow.

Brief Survival Guide

Office Gossip:

Develop multiple personality disorder

Take hallucinogenic drugs

Claim you have amnesia

Mass Hysterias

Today we are all going to:
Renounce all worldy possessions and move to the nearest rainforest

Answers to previous page

Brain Teaser: Answer = Cassius Clay
Piggy Bank: Answer = Asparagus
(he prefers fruits with more vowels in their name)

The One-Minute Philosopher

Here is a philosophical quote with the vowels (and "y's" and punctuation) removed and the letters put into groups of three. Can you decipher it?

HLL STH RPP L

Around the Water Cooler

You're all on short term contracts ■

No one's been paid yet ■

You're planning a walk-out ■

Ridiculous Rules

The head of any dead whale found on the British coast automatically becomes the property of the King, and the tail of the Queen.

In the Calendar

What happened on January 1, 45 B.C.?

Top Five

Best songs for calling in sick:

1. _____
2. _____
3. _____
4. _____
5. _____

Ballroom Blitz

Office chairs make excellent dancing partners.

Divide the players into dancers and judges.

Each dancer lines up (preferably dressed to impress).

You have two minutes to spin, glide and twirl your office chair in the most elegant and graceful style you can manage.

Judges award points for technical excellence and interpretation. The losers have to buy the winner a new outfit to wear to the company party. The winner must wear it no matter how hideous it is.

Guess the Phobia

Often happens on a Monday morning:

Pantophobia

Timewasters Synonymous

Find the missing word, which is closely related to the words on either side.

Then take the last letter of each word to make a new word.

Type   **** Arrange
Occasion **** Hour
Trade   **** Bargain
Phone   **** Summon

Clock Watching

How long is it until the 6:15 a.m. alarm call?

Morning Meditation

If you chase two rabbits, you will not catch either one.

Russian Proverb

Answers from previous page

In the Calendar: Answer = New Year's Day is celebrated the first time as the Julian calendar takes effect in Rome.
The One-Minute-Philosopher: Answer = "*Hell is other people*" (Sartre)

Payday for Optimists

Most of your salary has gone out in bank charges and overdraft fees but you've at least got two weeks before the whole charges thing sets in motion again.

Morning Meditation

If a placebo has an effect, is it any less real than the real thing?

Nathaniel LeTonnerre

Place Your Bets

_____'s wedding will be:

Sleek, expensive and stylish —/—

Raucous, drunken and wild —/—

Quiet, boring and uninspired —/—

Design Your Own

Lunch box:

Guess the Real Word

Bodillescious ☐

Boustrophedon ☐

Bognomania ☐

Change the Word

In 6 steps:

Merry

_____

_____

_____

_____

Waste

Named and Shamed

Boring _____

Bland _____

Bananas _____

Unlikely Candidate

Celebrity Chef _____

Mass Hysterias	In the Calendar
Today we are all going to: Wear our coats inside out as a representation of our internal thoughts.	Which was the first African colony to become an independent state?

Answers from previous page

Timewasters Synonymous: Answer = Tell (Sort, Time, Deal, Call)

Clock Watching: Answer = 4 hours and 45 minutes

Guess the Phobia: Answer = fear of everything

Word Fits

Complete these words using three four-letter words. In each group of three, the missing word is the same.

E X - - - -   S - - - -   E X C E L - - - -

- - - - A L   - - - - E N E D   - - - - I L

I M - - - - A N T   F O O L - - - - Y   P - - - - Y

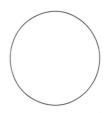
Whatever You Do

Don't even think about:

How long your day is, how tired you are

Heat rash under nylon clothing

Sewage spillage

Get the Job

Unscramble the anagram below to find the job.

Donor This Tot

Answer _____

Before They Were Famous

Colin Farrell has starred in many high-profile Hollywood films. But, do you know what he used to do for a living back in Ireland?

Answer _____

Extinct Jobs

Warrener:
A "warrener" looked after wild rabbit warrens keeping the rabbits safe from foxes, stoats and other predators. He killed and sold the rabbits for meat either door-to-door or at the local market.

Answers from previous page:

Change Word: Merry , Marry, Parry, Party, Pasty, Paste, Waste
In the Calendar: Answer = Liberia
Real Word: Answer = Boustrophedon (Of writing, alternating left to right then right to left.)

Domino Logic

What is the missing number?

=17

=24

=15

= ?

Payday for Optimists

You've just been mugged coming out of the bank. Still, you can feign "shock" and get a few days off work.

Breaktime Brain Teasers

He was an American Union General during the Civil War and was defeated at the Battle of Fredericksburg and the Battle of the Crater. He succeeded McClellan as Commander of the Union forces.
Who was this general?

Which Movie Contains the Following Quote?

"The point is, ladies and gentleman, that greed, for lack of a better word, is good. Greed is right, greed works. Greed clarifies, cuts through, and captures the essence of the evolutionary spirit."

Today's Target

To say "What?" happily to every question as if you haven't understood a word.

Top Ten

Transport to Work:

Car ☐
Airplane ☐
Boat ☐
Bicycle ☐
Walking ☐
Scooter ☐
Horseback ☐
Truck ☐
Hot air balloon ☐
Caravan ☐

Sing While You Work

Which song about work contains the following words?

They offered me the office, offered me the shop
They said I'd better take anything they'd got.

Answers from previous page

Get the Job: Answer = Orthodontist

Before They Were Famous: Answer = Colin Farrell was a line dance instructor

Word Fits: Answer = Port, Hard, Lent

Wordwheel

Using only the letters in the wordwheel, you have ten minutes to find as many words as possible, none of which may be plurals, foreign words or proper nouns. Each word must be of three letters or more, all must contain the central letter and letters can only be used once in every word.
There is at least one nine-letter word in the wheel.

Nine-letter word _____

Excuses for...

Your useless colleagues

_____

_____

_____

Work Face

Identity Theft

Word Mania

Can you see the one three-letter word which can be added on to these starting letters to make new words?

PL - - -

ST - - -

F - - -

M - - -

AB - - -

Thought for the Day

"The idle man does not know what it is to enjoy rest."
Albert Einstein

Answers from previous page

Sing While You Work: Answer = *Career Opportunities* The Clash

Movie quote: *Wall Street* (1987)

Brain Teaser: Answer = Ambrose Burnside

Dominoes: Answer = 20
(Just add the total spots on all three dominos together)

Ski Jumping

For this game, you need a roll of strong paper, such as packing paper. Tape or secure the roll to a box that is in turn attached to the floor.

Unroll the paper and attach the other end to a desk, which is higher than the box. The resulting shape should create a ski jump, so the paper slopes down from the desk, nearly, but not quite to the ground, then slopes up to the roll on the box.

Contestants take turns to choose items of office stationery such as pens, tape, staplers and so on. They place these at the top of the slope so they ski down the slope and are carried by momentum off the other end.

The winner is the player whose item jumps the furthest. The skill lies in trying to find items that are slippery enough and of the optimum weight so that they ski successfully.

Dice Man

Using three of the arithmetical signs +, −, X and ÷, can you achieve the correct total?

Payday for Optimists

Yes you're tired, but on Friday you can leave early. Maybe you'll be home by midnight?

Get the Job

Can you unscramble the anagram to reveal the job title?

Vernacular Bedim

Answer _____

Pick 'n' Mix

Choose 3 words to describe the the worst meeting:

Pointless Evil
Psychotic Brutal
Fear   Argument
Vicious   Embarrassing
Suspense   Laughter

Answers from previous page

Word Mania: Answer = Ate

Wordwheel nine-letter word = Secretary

The One-Minute Businessman

Here is a business catchphrase with the vowels (and "y's" and punctuation) removed and the letters put into groups of three. Can you decipher it?

BLS KTH NKN G

Today's Greatest Achievement

Clear-headed early morning ☐
First to the bar ☐
Clean, pressed pants ☐

Which Movie Contains the Following Quote?

"What we do know is we need a job. We need a high-paying job. Well, now we're too hot to be working anywhere in this country."

Work Face

○

Sleepless night

Top Five

Best songs for hiding from the boss:
1. _____
2. _____
3. _____
4. _____
5. _____

Breaktime Brain Teasers

Who is traditionally regarded as the discoverer of the "New World"?

Mind Games

Boss says: "I'm out for a meeting all afternoon."

Boss means: "I'm going home early."

Unlikely Candidate

Fashion Designer

_____

Answers from previous page

Get the Job: Answer = Ambulance Driver

Dice Man: Answer = 6 - 2 ÷ 4 + 3 = 4

Friday Night Sprint

This game is suitable for any night when you are planning after-work drinks.

There are two ways to play:

1. Each contestant has to attempt to be the first to leave work and reach the after-work venue, bar or club. In this form of the game, it becomes a strategy game, won by the player who is brazen enough to leave the earliest.

2. If you prefer to leave work on time, all players line up at the office door and, on a given signal, sprint to the venue.

In either case, the winner is entitled to free drinks, bought by the defeated players, all evening.

Place Your Bets

_____ 's outfit today will be:

Polka-dotted and peculiar	—/—
Stripy, strident and strict	—/—
Drab, dreary and dreadful	—/—

The Filing Cabinet

Which is the odd word out?

BATHHOUSE

HITCHHIKER

WITHHOLD

TREKKED

VACUUM

LEASEHOLD

GLOWWORM

Brief Survival Guide

Aggressive Boss:

1. Don't draw attention to yourself

2. Don't get caught doing anything

3. Don't go to work...

Answers from previous page

The One-Minute Businessman: Answer = Blue sky thinking

Movie Quote: Answer = *Ocean's Twelve (2004)*

Brain Teaser: Answer = Christopher Columbus

Trick Talk Detector

Your boss calls an emergency morning meeting to "think outside the box"

What is the real purpose of the meeting?

A: To try to get you to apply your mind to your work.

B: To organize a weekend "team-building" assault course.

C: To prove that he has more ideas than you do.

D: To set a trap that will show you have no idea what you're supposed to be doing.

Answer: Just come up with some whacky and wholly unsuitable ideas and he should let you go back to your burrow.

Ways to Pass the Time

Boring ☐

Blessing ☐

Beginning ☐

Design Your Own

Office party hat:

Piggy Bank

There is a special on at the cinema. Adults get $2.00 off their tickets if they bring a token from the local newspaper. Children also get a set reduction in the price of their tickets if they bring a token. On Saturday night, there are 100 adults and 60 children at the show. Half the adults get the discounted price, and a third of the children. The total cost of the discount to the cinema is $160. What was the discount for children who brought the token?

Today's Greatest Achievement

Right choice of alcohol ☐

Avoided getting wet ☐

Dispelling the argument ☐

In the Calendar

In what year did the Second World War start?

Answers from previous page

The Filing Cabinet: Answer = Leasehold (the others have a repeated consonant)

The Filing Cabinet

Which is the odd word out?

REVIVER
TUT-TUT
LOCAL
CIVIC
KAYAK
SAGAS

Who Am I?

Can you work out which singer's name is hidden in the anagram below?

PERSIST EARN BY

Work Face

Liquid lunch

Words to Impress Your Colleagues

Test yourself and expand your vocabulary.

Do you know the meaning of the word:

Fardel?

My Next Lunch Break

Late? _____

Early? _____

Non-existent _____

Today's Target

To get out of the office mid-morning without anyone noticing

Brief Survival Guide

Promotion:
1. Demand a large sum of money
2. Demand a new office and contents
3. Put your feet up...

Mass Hysterias

Today we are all going to...
Start a new religion worshipping computers

Answers from previous page

Piggy Bank: Answer = $3.00

In the Calendar: Answer = 1939

Wordwheel

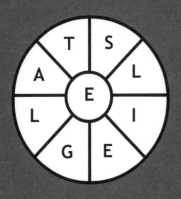

Using only the letters in the Wordwheel, you have ten minutes to find as many words as possible, none of which may be plurals, foreign words or proper nouns. Each word must be of three letters or more, all must contain the central letter and letters can only be used once in every word. There is at least one nine-letter word in the wheel.

Nine-letter word: _____

Ridiculous Rules

In the United Kingdom, Royal Navy ships that enter the Port of London must provide a barrel of rum to the Constable of the Tower of London.

Clock Watching

The boss is arriving at 4:15 p.m. How much longer?

Work Space

On March 29, 1974 Mariner 10 was the first spacecraft to fly by the planet Mercury. It sent back close-up pictures of a world that resembles our Moon.

Breaktime Brain Teasers

It created the world's first successful revolutionary state, but do you know in which year was the Russian Revolution?

Answer _____

Word Fits

Complete these words using three four-letter words. In each group of three, the missing word is the same.

- - - - A R   S P - - - -   F I T - - - -

F E - - - -   S T O - - - -   - - - - E R

I N C - - - - D   - - - - E R S   C O N - - - - A N T

Top Ten

Mid-morning Snack:

- Pies ☐
- Cakes ☐
- Cookies ☐
- Muffins ☐
- Trifle ☐
- Meringue ☐
- Ice-cream ☐
- Puddings ☐
- Pastries ☐
- Tarts ☐

Guess the Phobia

A definite after the office party:

Mnemophobia

Morning Meditation

Some people walk in the rain, others just get wet.

Roger Miller

In the Calendar

When did Albert Einstein publish his theory of relativity?

Paper Cup Magic

This is just as it sounds. Take five paper cups and turn them upside down. Put an eraser or pencil sharpener underneath one of the cups and swap them all around. Contestants must guess which paper cup the object is hidden under. The winner gets a free lunch.

Answers from previous page

Clock Watching: Answer = 4 hours and 55 minutes
Wordwheel nine-letter word: Legislate
Brain Teaser: Answer = 1917

Design Your Own

[blank box]

Boardroom Buffet

Unlikely Candidate

Psychic

_____

The Word Calculator

Find the alternative words that make this sum work:

IMMORAL ACT

+

RULER

_____

= DESCENDING

[Calculator with buttons: 1 2 3 0 +, 4 5 6 % -, 7 8 9 : =]

Whatever You Do

Don't even think about any of the following...

Missing teeth smile

Bare feet on sticky floors

Sunburned unmentionables

Get the Job

Unscramble the anagram below to find the job.

Monitor Gas

Answer _____

Before They Were Famous

We know him as an aging rocker but what job did Jon Bon Jovi do before he was famous?

Extinct Jobs

Fuller:

"Fullers" washed cloth (particularly wool), to take out any oils or impurities. During Roman times fullers were mainly slaves. Urine was used as a cleanser until the cleansing agent "fullers earth" was introduced in the medieval period.

Answers from previous page

In the Calendar: Answer = 1905

Guess the Phobia: Answer = Fear of memories

Word Fits: Answer = Line, Ring, Test

Payday for Optimists

Your wage makes no difference to the amount of debt you have but you've got a wardrobe full of lovely clothes.

Sing While You Work...

Which song about work do the lyrics below come from?

Loving you is driving me crazy
People say that you were
born lazy.

Domino Logic

Can you work out the missing number and the reason why?

= 21

= 35

= 13

= ?

Change the Word

In five steps...

Hear

_____

_____

_____

_____

Boom

Today's Target

Giggle helplessly every time the phone rings

Clock Watching

The meeting finishes at 1:30 p.m. How much longer?

Caught by the Boss

First to the bar ☐

Last man standing ☐

Hacking into his email ☐

Answers from previous page

Word Calculator: Answer = Sin (Immoral act) + King (Ruler) = Sinking (Descending)

Get the Job: Answer = Agronomist

Before They Were Famous: Jon Bon Jovi made Christmas decorations

WORDWHEEL

Using only the letters in the Wordwheel, you have ten minutes to find as many words as possible, none of which may be plurals, foreign words or proper nouns. Each word must be of three letters or more, all must contain the central letter and letters can only be used once in every word.

There is at least one nine-letter word in the wheel.

Nine-letter word _____

Today's Target

To double up with laughter every time you see your boss

The One-Minute Comedian

Here is a humorous quote with the vowels (and "y"s and punctuation) removed and the letters put into groups of three. Can you decipher it?

VHD PRF CTL WND RFL
VNN GBT THS WSN TT

Thought For the Day

One must work and dare if one really wants to live.
Vincent van Gogh

Answers from previous page

Domino Logic: Answer = 51 (Multiply the total spots on the first domino by the total spots on the third, then subtract the total spots on the second domino)

Clock Watching: Answer = 4 hours and 15 minutes

Change the Word: Duel, Dull, Bull, Ball, Bale, Bile, Vile

Sing While You Work: *Work Is A Four-Letter Word* The Smiths

Dice Man

Using three of the arithmetical signs
+, -, x and ÷,
can you achieve the correct total?

Payday for Pessimists

This month you really, really will resign
(but you haven't managed to find another
job yet).

Word Fits

Complete these words using three four-
letter words. In each group of three,
the missing word is the same.

```
S - - - - I N G
- - - - I E R
A N T - - - -

H O - - - -
- - - - I N G
E A R - - - -

B - - - -
D - - - - E R
C - - - - E D
```

Lunchtime Sudoku

4		9		7		3		1
	2				3				4
		8		4		2		9	
5		3	1		4	8		2
	4		8		7		3	
8		7	3		5	4		6
	1		2		3		6	
6				8				7
9		8		5		1		3

Get the Job

Can you unscramble
the anagram below
to get the job title?

Rather Hog Pop

Answer _____

Pick 'n' Mix

Choose 3 words to
describe a first
day at work:

Fun	Drink
Interesting	Food
Boring	Hopeful
Scary	Dreadful
Happy	Laughing

Answers from previous page

Wordwheel nine-letter word: Franchise
The One-Minute Commedian: Answer =
"I've had a perfectly wonderful evening.
But this wasn't it." (Groucho Marx)

Top Ten

Lunch-time Excercise:

- Run ☐
- Walk ☐
- Crawl ☐
- Skip ☐
- Jump ☐
- Leap ☐
- Hop ☐
- Stroll ☐
- Creep ☐
- Jog ☐

Board Meeting Doodle

Place Your Bets

You ask for some more money because:

You need to make a quick getaway —/—

You need a drink —/—

You've never had any —/—

Named and Shamed

Psychobabbler _____

New age hipster _____

Hippy dippy hanger-on _____

The Filing Cabinet

Which is the odd word out?

GYPSY

FLYS

CRYING

RHYTHM

SPRY

NYMPH

Whatever You Do

Don't even think about
any of the following:

Hideously bad breath

Imminent travel sickness

Broken furniture

Answers from previous page

Word Fits: Answer = Hill, Nest, Ream

Lunchtime Sudoku:

4	5	9	6	7	8	3	2	1
2	7	1	5	3	9	6	8	4
3	8	6	4	1	2	7	9	5
5	6	3	1	9	4	8	7	2
1	4	2	8	6	7	5	3	9
8	9	7	3	2	5	4	1	6
7	1	5	2	4	3	9	6	8
6	3	4	9	8	1	2	5	7
9	2	8	7	5	6	1	4	3

Get the Job:
Answer = Photographer

Dice Man:
Answer = 2 x 6 - 2 ÷ 5 = 2

Ways to Pass the Time

Dreaming ☐

Dodging ☐

Loafing ☐

Design Your Own

Company flag

The Word Calculator

Find the alternative words that make this sum work:

DAMAGE

+ FEWER

―――――――

= INNOCUOUS
―――――――

1	2	3	0	+
4	5	6	%	-
7	8	9	÷	=

Brain Teaser

The term "Old World" was used to refer to Europe, Asia and Africa. Where does the term "New World" refer to?

Piggy Bank

The deadline for tax returns is the end of the month that comes three months after the month two months before the month after last month.

When do you have to complete the tax return?

Two-Word Horoscopes

Aries - Losing bet   Libra - Crawl in

Taurus - Later fun   Scorpio - Not clever

Gemini - No worries   Sagittarius - Happy pants

Cancer - Not now   Capricorn - Telephone them

Leo - Isolated incident   Aquarius - Be organized

Virgo - Keep out   Pisces - New shoes

Answers from previous page

The Filing Cabinet: Answer = Crying
(the other words contain no proper vowels, only "y's")

Who Am I?

Which singer's name is hidden in the anagram below?

I Hurricane a slag it

Work Face

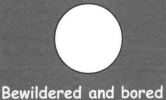

Bewildered and bored

The Filing Cabinet

Which is the odd word out?

CATCHPHRASE

LATCHSTRING

STRETCHMARKS

SIGHTSCREEN

WATCHSPRING

KNIGHTSBRIDGE

Words to impress your colleagues

Test yourself and expand your vocabulary
Do you know the meaning of the word:

Saccadic?

Sing While You Work

These lyrics are from a song about work.
Can you guess the song?

I got no time for livin'
Yes, I'm workin' all the time

Today's Target

Only speak when the clock strikes the hour and remain silent at other times.

Brief Survival Guide

Office Arguments:

Shout loudest

Shout angriest

Shout last...

Mass Hysterias

Today we are all going to:
Wash our feet in spring water and give praise to the storm clouds.

Answers to previous page

Brain Teaser: Answer = The Americas and Australasia
Piggy Bank: Answer = The end of next month
The Word Calculator: Answer = (Damage) Harm + (Fewer) Less = (Innocuous) Harmless

Timewasters Synonymous

Find the missing word, which is closely related to the words on either side.
Then take the third letter of each word to make a new word.

Gravel **** Bravery
Fee **** Chime
Sign **** Inform

Unlikely Candidate

Best Dressed

_____

Around the Water Cooler

Company merger   ▮

Industrial espionage   ▮

Computer worm   ▮

Work Space

Olympus Mons, a volcano found on Mars, is the largest volcano found in our solar system. It is 370 miles (595 km) across and rises 15 miles (24 km).

In the Calendar

What happened on August 1, 1914?

Top Five

Best songs for being fired:

1. _____
2. _____
3. _____
4. _____
5. _____

Domino Logic

What is the missing number?

🁣 | 🁢 | 🁩 = 122010

🁧 | 🁡 | 🁥 = 121101

🁦 | 🁨 | 🁟 = 111111

🁤 | 🁦 | 🁝 = ?

Change the Word

Beats to Truth in 6 steps:

Beats

_____

_____

_____

_____

_____

Truth

Guess the Phobia

When you hope no one notices your mistakes:

Phronemophobia

Brief Survival Guide

Team Building Course:

Fake a broken leg

Fake a debilitating illness

Fake mental incapacity

Clock Watching

Coffee break is at 10:00 a.m. How much longer?

Morning Meditation

Sometimes it's necessary to go a long distance out of the way in order to come back a short distance correctly.
Edward Albee

Answers from previous page

In the Calendar: Answer = Outbreak of the First World War

Timewasters Snonymous: Answer = Ill (Grit, Toll, Tell)

Payday for Optimists

You only earn enough for your rent, food and bills, but then again you have no social life so new outfits aren't necessary.

Morning Meditation

There are some remedies worse than the disease.

Publilius Syrus

Design Your Own

Coffee cup:

Guess the Real Word

Carfax ☐

Calynorpious ☐

Caldivering ☐

Change the Word

In 6 steps:

Flash

_____

_____

_____

_____

Bling

Place Your Bets

Your chair collapsed because:

You're very drunk   —/—

You've broken it   —/—

It had no legs   —/—

Named and Shamed

Obvious liar   _____

Worst nightmare   _____

Dictator   _____

Unlikely Candidate

Senator   _____

Mass Hysterias

Today we are all going to:

Dye our hair a crazy color.

In the Calendar

What happened on December 25, 1223?

Answers from previous page

Change the Word: Answer = Beats, Boats, Boots, Booth, Tooth, Troth, Truth

Clock Watching: Answer = 1 hour and 40 minutes

Guess the Phobia: Answer = fear of thinking

Domino Logic: Answer =130011 (The first digit in the six digit answer is based on how many times a 1 is used on the row, the second digit is based on how many times a 2 is used etc.

Word Fits

Complete these words using three four letter words. In each group of three, the missing word is the same.

S - - - - I N G   H O - - - -   B - - - -
- - - - I E R   - - - - I N G   D - - - - E R
A N T - - - -   E A R - - - -   C - - - - E D

Work Face

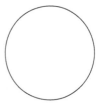

Stock Market Crash

Unlikely Candidate

Saint

_____

Whatever You Do

Don't even think about any of the following:

Broken mirrors under your feet

Splinters in your fingers

Loose floorboards on the top floor

Get the Job

Unscramble the anagram below to find the job.

Gene Rein

Answer _____

Before They Were Famous

We know him as a Hollywood superstar but what job did Warren Beatty have before he was famous?

Answer _____

Extinct Jobs

Costermonger:

"Costermongers" sold fruit and vegetables from a barrow in a typical street market in Victorian times, often shouting the prices loudly to out-do any rivals.

Answers from previous page:

Change Word: Flash, Flask, Flank, Blank, Bland Blind, Bling
In the Calendar: Answer = St. Francis of Assisi assembled first Nativity scene in Greccio, Italy
Real Word: Answer = Carfax is the place where four roads meet

Domino Logic

What is the missing number?

 = 1

 = 2

=1

= ?

Payday for Optimists

Pay raise! Pay raise! (You secretly think human resources has got it wrong but don't say anything).

Breaktime Brain Teasers

What president was eulogized as, "First in war, first in peace, and first in the hearts of his countrymen"?

Which Movie Contains the Following Quote?

"Looks like you've been missing a lot of work lately."

"I wouldn't say I've been missing it, Bob."

Today's Target

To hop across the office on one leg every time you need to move.

Top Ten

Vacations:

Seashore ☐
Woodland ☐
City ☐
Prairie ☐
Riverside ☐
Mountains ☐
Countryside ☐
Lakes ☐
Desert ☐
Forest ☐

Sing While You Work

Which song about work contains the following words?

Work work work if you want
to improve it
Push it along

Answers from previous page

Get the Job: Answer = Engineer

Before They Were Famous:
Answer = Warren Beatty worked as a rat catcher.

Word Fits: Answer = Hill, Nest, Ream

Wordwheel

Using only the letters in the wordwheel, you have ten minutes to find as many words as possible, none of which may be plurals, foreign words or proper nouns. Each word must be of three letters or more, all must contain the central letter and letters can only be used once in every word.
There is at least one nine-letter word in the wheel.

Nine-letter word _____

Excuses for...

Idling on the internet

_____

Work Face

Office tantrum

Word Fits

Complete these words using two three-letter words. In each group of four, the missing word is the same.

S T - - -   S H - - -
- - - A   H - - - S T
P - - - N T   A L - - -
W - - - H O U S E   C - - -

Thought for the Day

The harder I work the more I live.
George Bernard Shaw

File Skateboarding

For this game, you need file folders that are slippery when on the office carpet. You will also need to clear a "run" in the office where participants can slide on their files.

All partcipants must choose their folders and place them on the floor a few feet in front of them.

Contestants need to run to their file and jump onto it with both feet to make it start to slide.

The winner is the contestant who manages to slide the furthest.

Dice Man

Using three of the arithmetical signs +, −, X and ÷, can you achieve the correct total?

Payday for Pessimists

All that money but you're too tired to enjoy it.

Get the Job

Can you unscramble the anagram to reveal the job title?

Brain Liar

Answer _____

Pick 'n' Mix

Choose 3 words to describe your team leader:

Friendship Stupid
Masochistic Sadistic
Fighting Commitment
Caring Understanding
Argumentative Fun

Answers from previous page

Word Fits: Answer = Are, One

Wordwheel nine-letter Word:
Answer = Eccentric

Timewasters Synonymous

Find the missing word, which is closely related to the words on either side.

Then take the last letter of each word to make a new word.

Naked **** Unadorned
Drill **** Dull
Hill **** Descended

Today's Greatest Achievement

Matching socks for once ▪

Not tripping over the cat ▪

Subordination ▪

Which Movie Contains the Following Quote?

"What if I told you insane was working fifty hours a week in some office for fifty years at the end of which they tell you to piss off; ending up in some retirement village, hoping to die before suffering the indignity of trying to make it to the toilet on time? Wouldn't you consider that to be insane?"

Work Face

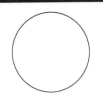

Headache

Top Five

Best songs for a business lunch:

1. _____
2. _____
3. _____
4. _____
5. _____

Breaktime Brain Teasers

It has become an essential part of modern economics and administration, but do you know in what year the watch was invented?

Mind Games

Boss says:
"I hate to be the bearer of bad news."
Boss means: "Thank goodness I can now get rid of you."

Unlikely Candidate

High Brow

_____

Answers from previous page

Get the Job: Answer = Librarian

Dice Man: Answer = 4 x 5 - 5 ÷ 3 = 5

Hunt the Company Credit Card

Choose one person to hide the company credit card.

While the card is being hidden, all other participants must close their eyes or be blindfolded.

The chosen player should hide the card in a place where it will be hard to find. When it is hidden he or she must then tell the rest of the participants to open their eyes and look for the card.

The winner is the person who finds the card and must get free drinks all evening.

Place Your Bets

_____ 's party outfit will be:

Cheap, sparkly and ridiculous   —/—

Cool, elegant and tasteful   —/—

Mutton-dressed-as-lamb   —/—

The Filing Cabinet

Which is the odd word out?

SCRATCH
CAUGHT
STRENGTH
BORSCHT
SCRAMS
FLIGHTS

Brief Survival Guide

Job Interview:

1. **Rehearse over-eager workaholic persona the night before**

2. **Try to remember what the job description is**

3. **Wash and dress before going**

Answers from previous page

Timewasters Synonymous: Answer = Eel (Bare, Bore, Fell)

Movie Quote: Answer = *Con Air* (1997)

Brain Teaser: Answer = 1509

Trick Talk Detector

Your boss announces that he's doing a "gap analysis."

What is really going on?

A: He wants to get rid of some employees

B: He's testing how loyal you are to him

C: He wants new windows in his office

Answer: Immediately ask if he needs help with anything.

Ways to pass the Time

Enjoying ☐

Complaining ☐

Grumbling ☐

Design Your Own

Bathroom poster:

Piggy Bank

In the piggy bank there is a mixture of $10, $5 , $2 and $1 dollar bills.

There is at least one of each type of bill.

On counting the money you find that you have $283 exactly.

There are 31 bills altogether.

How many $5 dollar bills do you have?

Today's Greatest Achievement

Subterfuge at your desk ☐

Saving money for your bills ☐

Displaying a vicious temper ☐

In the Calendar

In what year was the British tea-carrying ship the *Cutty Sark* built?

Answers from previous page

The Filing Cabinet: Answer = Caught has two vowels, (the others have only one)

The Word Calculator

Find the alternative words that make this sum work:

BEGIN

+

DIRECTED

_____

= SURPRISED

Who Am I?

Can you work out which singer's name is hidden in the anagram below?

REPRESENT SING CUB

Work Face

Big trouble

Words to Impress Your Colleagues

Test yourself and expand your vocabulary.

Do you know the meaning of the word:

Jactancy?

My Next Job

Title _____

Responsibility _____

Salary _____

Today's Target

To do absolutely no work all day without getting caught.

Brief Survival Guide

Lunch with Colleagues:

1. Avoid sitting next to the show-off

2. Avoid eating messily

3. Avoid going

Mass Hysterias

Today we are all going to...
Lock ourselves in the stationery room to avoid a meeting

Answers from previous page

Piggy Bank: Answer = 2

In the Calendar: Answer = 1869

Wordwheel

Using only the letters in the Wordwheel, you have ten minutes to find as many words as possible, none of which may be plurals, foreign words or proper nouns. Each word must be of three letters or more, all must contain the central letter and letters can only be used once in every word. There is at least one nine-letter word in the wheel.

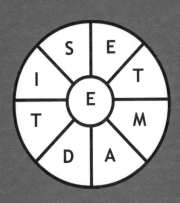

Nine-letter word: _____

Ridiculous Rules

This shouldn't come as much of a surprise but apparently, in Alabama, it is illegal for a driver to be blindfolded while driving a vehicle.

Breaktime Brain Teasers

His plays were a hit during the days of Queen Elizabeth I but in what year was playwright William Shakespeare born?

Answer _____

Clock Watching

The late shift ends at 8:00 p.m. How long until then?

Work Space

Driving at 75 miles (121 km) per hour, it would take 258 days to drive around one of Saturn's rings.

Answers from previous page

The Word Calculator: Answer = (Begin) Start + (Directed) Led = (Surprised) Startled

Who Am I? Answer = Bruce Springsteen

Impress Your Colleagues: Answer = Jactancy means boastfulness.

Dice Man

Using three of the arithmetical signs
+, -, x and ÷,
can you achieve the correct total?

Top Ten

Argument with Colleague:

- Shout ☐
- Sing ☐
- Talk ☐
- Laugh ☐
- Yell ☐
- Whisper ☐
- Yodel ☐
- Cry ☐
- Recite ☐
- Sigh ☐

Guess the Phobia

When your desk drawer makes you cringe:

Ataxophobia

Morning Meditation

It is easy to stand a pain, but difficult to stand an itch

Chang Ch'ao

In the Calendar

In what year did Christopher Columbus discover the New World?

Desk Top Ski Race

Each player must make a skiing figure out of rolled up paper or sticky tape. Using available files and other paraphanlia from your desk create a ski run. Each palyer must line their skiing figures up at the top of the ski run then on a count of three let them go. The winner is the player whose ski figure goes the furthest or the first to reach the end of the run.

Answers from previous page

Clock Watching: Answer = 11 hours and 10 minutes
Wordwheel nine-letter word: Estimated
Brain Teaser: Answer = 1564

Design Your Own

Staff re-shuffle

Unlikely Candidate

Body Builder

_____

The Word Calculator

Find the alternative words that make this sum work:

SMASH

+

QUICK

_____

=   **MEAL**

_____

Whatever You Do

Don't even think about any of the following:

- The smell of strong cheese
- Squeaky gates in the night
- Wasp stings on sensitive areas

Get the Job

Unscramble the anagram below to find the job.

Ballet Roof

Answer _____

Before They Were Famous

Ashton Kutcher has "Punk'd" many on his MTV hit show but what was his job before he became famous?

Extinct Jobs

Wainwright and Wheelwright:

"Wainwrights" made wagons that would have been pulled by horses. "Wain" is an old name for wagon.

The "wheelwright" made the wagon's wheels.

Answers from previous page

In the Calendar: Answer = 1492

Guess the Phobia: Answer = Fear of untidiness

Dice Man: Answer = 6 + 5 - 3 ÷ 2 = 4

Payday for Optimists

You've just been paid but your TV has broken down. Still, you can now read all those books you're been meaning to read.

Sing While You Work...

Which song about work do the lyrics below come from?

Five days out of seven
eight hours of every one
I'm tryin' to buy a piece
of heaven

Domino Logic

Can you work out the missing number and the reason why?

 = 9

= 12

= 9

= ?

Change the Word

In six steps...

Duel

_____

_____

_____

_____

_____

Vile

Today's Target

Yawn loudly every time someone asks you to do something

Clock Watching

The afternoon break is at 4:10 p.m. How long do you have to wait?

Caught by the Boss

Out drinking when you called in sick ☐

Out shopping when you called in sick ☐

Out.............................but sick ☐

Answers from previous page

Word Calculator:
Answer = (Smash) Break + (Quick) Fast = (Meal) Breakfast

Get the Job: Answer = Footballer

Before They Were Famous: Ashton Kutcher was once a biochemical engineer.

WORDWHEEL

Using only the letters in the Wordwheel, you have ten minutes to find as many words as possible, none of which may be plurals, foreign words or proper nouns. Each word must be of three letters or more, all must contain the central letter and letters can only be used once in every word.
There is at least one nine-letter word in the wheel.

Nine-letter word _____

Word Fits

Complete these words using three four-letter words. In each group of three, the missing word is the same.

- - - - S T   S - - - - S

S - - - -   - - - - I N G

- - - - Y   U N S - - - - E D

A - - - - M E N T

- - - - U M

B E - - - -

Answers from previous page

Domino Logic: Answer = 8
(The highest total number of spots on any domino in that row)

Clock Watching: Answer = 4 hours and 15 minutes

Change the Word:

Duel, Dull, Bull, Ball, Bale, Bile, Vile

Sing While You Work: Answer = *Work* Leo Sayer

Dice Man

Using three of the arithmetical signs
+, -, x and ÷,
can you achieve the correct total?

Payday for Pessimists

You hate your job...you hate your job...
you hate your job.

Word Fits

Complete these words using three four
letter words. In each group of three,
the missing word is the same.

Q U - - -
F - - - E R
T - - -
- - - N E S S

H - - - Y
S T - - -
W - - - E R
L - - -

Lunchtime Sudoku

	3			8				9
		9	4		2		7	
		7	5		1	6	2	
		1			9		8	9
		6		1		4		
5	2		7			3		
	9	4	1		5	8		
	5		3		6	9		
7				4			6	

Get the Job

Can you unscramble
the anagram below
to get the job title?

The Arctic

Answer _____

Pick 'n' Mix

Choose 3 words to
describe your last
job interview:

Fear   Calm

Taxing   Capable

Confidence   Clever

Hopeless   Horrible

Panic   Humiliating

Top Ten

Work-Avoidance Aids:

- Book ☐
- Magazine ☐
- Leaflet ☐
- Poster ☐
- Newspaper ☐
- Comic book ☐
- Pamphlet ☐
- Picture book ☐
- Letter ☐
- Postcard ☐

Board Meeting Doodle

Place Your Bets

A dark sky means:

A storm is brewing —/—

It's night time —/—

You're wearing sunglasses —/—

Named and Shamed

Obvious liar _____

Worst nightmare _____

Dictator _____

Timewasters Synonymous

Find the missing word, which is closely related to the words on either side.

Then take the third letter of each word to make a new word.

Strongbox **** Secure

Fashionable **** Mild

Expensive **** Beloved

Season **** Descend

Whatever You Do

Don't even think about any of the following:

Sheep's eyes in your soup

Burnt hair on car seats

Ice burns on your tongue

Answers from previous page

Lunchtime Sudoku:

Get the Job:
Answer = Architect

Dice Man:
Answer = 2 x 3 + 4 - 5 = 5

Word Fits: Answer = Ill, And

2	3	5	6	8	7	1	4	9
1	6	9	4	3	2	5	7	8
4	8	7	5	9	1	6	2	3
3	4	1	2	5	9	7	8	6
9	7	6	8	1	3	4	5	2
5	2	8	7	6	4	3	9	1
6	9	4	1	2	5	8	3	7
8	5	2	3	7	6	9	1	4
7	1	3	9	4	8	2	6	5

Ways to Pass the Time

Rollerblading ☐
Cycling ☐
Skateboarding ☐

Design Your Own

Company curtains

The Word Calculator

Find the alternative words that make this sum work:

$$\begin{aligned} &\text{CIRCUIT} \\ + \ &\text{CROON} \\ \hline = \ &\text{ERRING} \end{aligned}$$

Brain Teaser

What is the name of the dam on the River Zambia at the Zimbabwe border?

Piggy Bank

In the piggy bank there is a mixture of $10, $5 , $2 and $1 dollar bills.
There is at least one of each type of bill.
On counting the money you find that you have $36 exactly.
There are 22 bills altogether.
How many $1 dollar bills do you have?

Two-Word Horoscopes

Aries - On television
Taurus - White socks
Gemini - Don't tell
Cancer - Daisy chain
Leo - Get away
Virgo - Grow up

Libra - Give up
Scorpio - Lie down
Sagittarius - Happy accident
Capricorn - You rock!
Aquarius - Back home?
Pisces - Not this

Answers from previous page

Timewasters Synonymous: Answer = Foal
(Safe, Cool, Dear, Fall)

Who Am I?

Which singer's name is hidden in the anagram below?

Murder on song

Work Face

Jealous and vindictive

Word Fits

Complete these words using two three letter words.
In each group of four, the missing word is the same.

S H R - - -   F - - -

- - - Y   W - - - Y

T H - - - E R   H - - - I N G

C L - - -   - - - N I N G

Words to Impress Your Colleagues

Test yourself and expand your vocabulary
Do you know the meaning of the word?:

Palter?

Sing While You Work

These lyrics are from a song about work.
Can you guess the song?

Muscle an' blood an' skin an' bone
A mind that's weak and a back that's strong

Today's Target

Re-enact a scene from a musical as an answer to any question you're asked

Brief Survival Guide

Junior Training:

Practice saying "no" a lot

Add whisky to afternoon coffee

Send to local stores on frequent errands

Mass Hysterias

Today we are all going to:
Abandon the dirty dishes and let mice lick our plates clean instead

Answers to previous page

Brain Teaser: Answer = The Kariba Dam
Piggy Bank: Answer = 19
The Word Calculator: Answer = (Circuit) Lap +
(Croon) Sing = (Erring) Lapsing

Timewasters Synonymous

Find the missing word, which is closely related to the words on either side.
Then take the third letter of each word to make a new word.

Zenith **** Tip
Summon **** Ice
Grinder **** Factory

Unlikely Candidate

Wedding of the Year

_____

Around the Water Cooler

Witch hunt	■
Scapegoat	■
Whipping boy	■

Work Space

If you attempted to count all the stars in a galaxy at a rate of one every second it would take around 3,000 years to count them all.

In the Calendar

What happened in France in 1789?

Top Five

Best songs for returning your tax forms:
1. _____
2. _____
3. _____
4. _____
5. _____

Domino Logic

Can you work out the missing number and the reason why?

(dominoes) = 2

(dominoes) = 1

(dominoes) = 3

(dominoes) = ?

Change the Word

In 6 steps:

Thumb

_____
_____
_____
_____
_____

Crass

Guess the Phobia

When the greetings cards come round:

Athazagoraphobia

Brief Survival Guide

Office Party:

Start early on the cocktails

Finish late with the whisky

Stuff enough food into your mouth to avoid having to speak

Clock Watching

Coffee break is at 10:00 a.m. How much longer?

Morning Meditation

No matter where you go or what you do, you live your entire life within the confines of your head.

Terry Josephson

Answers from previous page

In the Calendar: Answer = The French Revolution

Timewasters Snonymous: Answer = Ail (Peak, Hail, Mill)

Payday for Optimists

How generous your boss is to have given you an extra few dollars for working until midnight all week.

Morning Meditation

The fly that doesn't want to be swatted is most secure when it lights on the fly-swatter.

G.C. Lichtenberg

Design Your Own

Watch tower:

Guess the Real Word

Deitantious	☐
Dittany	☐
Diaglyph	☐

Change the Word

In 6 steps:

Sick

_____

_____

_____

_____

_____

Done

Place Your Bets

In your office there is:

Beautiful flowers and shrubs	—/—
An old sofa and a couple of tables	—/—
Who knows, you haven't been in it this year	—/—

Named and Shamed

Attention seeker	_____
Spoiled brat	_____
Off the rails	_____

Unlikely Candidate

Mayor _____

Mass Hysterias	Mind Games
Today we are all going to: Leap over walls rather than use the gates	Boss says: "Let's discuss it later." Boss means: "I have no intention of ever discussing it with you."

Answers from previous page

Change the Word: Answer = Thumb, Thump, Trump, Tramp, Cramp, Crams, Crass

Clock Watching: Answer = 1 hour and 40 minutes

Guess the Phobia: Answer = Fear of being forgotten

Domino Logic: Answer = 2 (the left hand side of the next domino that can be played in the game)

Word Fits

Complete these words using three four letter words. In each group of three, the missing word is the same.

BE - - - D
- - - GE
- - - S
SUL - - - D

- - - K
EF - - - T
- - - MED
- - - TH

Work Face

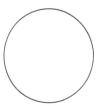

Big breakfast

Unlikely Candidate

Federal judge

_____

Whatever You Do

Don't even think about any of the following:

Boils all over your body

Major surgery with local anaesthetic

Raw liver in a plastic bag

Get the Job

Unscramble the anagram below to find the job.

INSECT SIT

Answer _____

Before They Were Famous

She is now a Hollywood movie star but what job did Jennifer Jason Leigh do before she was famous?

Answer _____

Guess the Real Word

Which is the real word?

Episemon ☐

Electonscious ☐

Eelogometry ☐

Answers from previous page:

Change the Word: Sick, Sink, Wink, Wine, Dine, Done

Guess the Real Word: Answer = Diaglyph (A figure etched or engraved into a flat surface of a gem, stone or other object.)

Domino Logic

What is the missing number?

(domino puzzle) = 5

(domino puzzle) = 4

(domino puzzle) = 6

(domino puzzle) = ?

Payday for Optimists

It is bonus day but you've just crashed the car. Have a celebratory drink and walk home instead.

Breaktime Brain Teasers

Which song did HAL the computer sing before he was deactivated in the film 2001?

Which Movie Contains the Following Quote?

"The worst thing about business is that it makes you feel old and look old."

Today's Target

To put your head on your desk and stay like that all day

Top Ten

Lunchtime Shopping:

Book store ☐
Clothes shop ☐
News stand ☐
Grocers ☐
Butchers ☐
Market ☐
Boutique ☐
Fishmongers ☐
Candy store ☐
Bakery ☐

Sing While You Work

Which song about work contains the following words?

A perfect day to get out of bed
Shower, dress, shave, kiss you on the head
Then I hit the office and my head starts to swim

Answers from previous page

Real Word: Answer = Episemon (A badge or characteristic device.)
Get the Job: Answer = Scientist
Before They Were Famous:
Answer = Jennifer Jason Leigh wrapped gifts in a store.
Word Fits: Answer = Lie, For

Wordwheel

Using only the letters in the wordwheel, you have ten minutes to find as many words as possible, none of which may be plurals, foreign words or proper nouns. Each word must be of three letters or more, all must contain the central letter and letters can only be used once in every word.

There is at least one nine-letter word in the wheel.

Nine-letter word _____

Word Fits

Complete these words using two three-letter words. In each group of four, the missing word is the same.

- - - E   C O - - -
- - - T E S T   - - - I E R
S - - - E   - - - A L
- - - I F E R   - - - H A N E

Excuses for...

Not answering the phone:

_____

_____

_____

Work Face

New supervisor

Thought for the Day

Talent is cheaper than table salt. What separates the talented individual from the successful one is a lot of hard work.
Stephen King

Answers from previous page

Sing While You Work: Answer = *Don't Talk To Me About Work* Lou Reed

Movie Quote: *Notorious* (1946)

Brain Teaser: Answer = *A Bicycle Built for Two*

Domino Logic: Answer = 6
(the sum of the spots of each domino in the row)

File Figure Skating

Three to five office workers must be appointed as judges and given cards numbered one to nine.

Each participant needs two files and two large rubber bands

Attach one file to each foot using the rubber bands and create a 'skating' arena on the office/workroom floor.

Each participant must practise a skating sequence that lasts for approximately two minutes.

The judges then each award points for how good they thought the routine and skill was. The winner is the one with the most points.

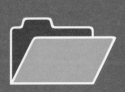

Dice Man

Using three of the arithmetical signs +, −, X and ÷ can you achieve the correct total?

Payday for Pessimists

The money's OK but you'd rather die than do this job another day.

Get the Job

Can you unscramble the anagram to reveal the job title?

Chirpily Nutcases

Answer _____

Pick 'n' Mix

Choose 3 words to describe your boss:

Dictatorial Stupid
Understanding Daft
Considerate Scary
Angry Domineering
Egotist Intelligence

Answers from previous page

Word Fits: Answer = Con, Met

Wordwheel nine-letter word: Swindling

Timewasters Synonymous

Find the missing word, which is closely related to the words on either side.

Then take the last letter of each word to make a new word.

Peninsula ** Cloak**
Metal ** Flatten**
Cram ** Satiate**
Fish ** Only**

Today's Greatest Achievement

Serenity in a crisis ▪

A wider chest ▪

Winning the argument ▪

Which Movie Contains the Following Quote?

"I worked for this old man and once he told me that he had spent his whole life thinking about his career and his work. And he was fifty-two and it suddenly struck him that he had never really given anything of himself. His life was for no one and nothing."

Work Face

○

Repetetive Strain Injury

Top Five

Best songs for singing while you work:

1. _____
2. _____
3. _____
4. _____
5. _____

Breaktime Brain Teasers

Which former U.S. Attorney General and Presidential Candidate was assassinated in a hotel's kitchen?

Mind Games

Boss says: "You will not be affected by the merger."

Boss means: "You may lose your job."

Unlikely Candidate

Police Chief

_____

Answers from previous page

Get the Job: Answer = Nuclear Physicist

Dice Man: Answer = 1 + 1 x 3 ÷ 1 = 6

Desk Surfing

Clear spaces across a number of desks.

For this game you will need a watch or clock with a second hand.

Each player starts off at the first desk then moves onto the second and subsequent desks without touching the floor.

Each player must be timed as he or she completes the desk surf course without touching the floor.

The winner is the player who surfs all desks without touching the floor in the fastest time.

Place Your Bets

_____ 's birthday party will be:

Crazy as usual   —/—

A minimal sober affair   —/—

Soon abandoned   —/—

The Filing Cabinet

Which is the odd word out?

ORYX
ECHIDNA
ORACLE
OKAPI
CASSOWARY

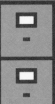

Brief Survival Guide

Business Traveling:

Don't forget tickets and passports

Prepare for a horrible hotel

Try to remember what your destination is

Trick Talk Detector

Your boss announces that he wants to "repurpose" you.

What does he really mean?

A: He wants to give you something new to do.

B: He wants to give you a lobotomy.

C: He thinks you're pointless.

Answer: Deny everything and insist that you're happy as you are.

Ways to Pass the Time

Hiding ☐

Hollering ☐

Hounding ☐

Design Your Own

Message board:

Word Fits

Complete these words using two three-letter words. In each group of four, the missing word is the same.

```
B R - - -        W H - - -
- - - E D        R - - - S
C - - - S        F - - - I N G
- - - Y          R - - - E C T
```

Today's Greatest Achievement

A slimmer waist ☐

Finding new route home ☐

Brushing hair ☐

In the Calendar

In 1945, two cities were the main targets for V-2 rockets. Which cities were they?

Answers from previous page

The Filing Cabinet: Answer = Oracle
(the others are names of animals)

The Word Calculator

Find the alternative words that make this sum work:

BLEMISH

+

DRINK

= EDGE

1	2	3	0	+
4	5	6	%	-
7	8	9	÷	=

Who Am I?

Can you work out which singer's name is hidden in the anagram below?

CLEVER NOT YOU

Work Face

Gossip monger

Words to Impress Your Colleagues

Test yourself and expand your vocabulary.

Do you know the meaning of the word:

Nanocephalous?

My Next Argument

Who _____

Why _____

Where _____

Today's Target

To sing your answer when anyone asks you a question

Brief Survival Guide

Asking for a date:

1. Avoid looking overly eager
2. Pretend you don't really care
3. Just be nice!

Mass Hysterias

Today we are all going to...
Cover ourselves with a blanket and hope that no one notices us.

Answers from previous page

Word Fits: Answer = Oil, Eel

In the Calendar: Answer = London and Antwerp

Wordwheel

Using only the letters in the Wordwheel, you have ten minutes to find as many words as possible, none of which may be plurals, foreign words or proper nouns. Each word must be of three letters or more, all must contain the central letter and letters can only be used once in every word. There is at least one nine-letter word in the wheel.

Nine-letter word: _____

Ridiculous Rules

In Florida, women can be fined for falling asleep under a dryer at a hair salon. Apparently the salon owners can also be fined.

Clock Watching

Lunch is at 1:00 p.m., and it is four times as long to the end of the day as to lunch

When does the day end?

Breaktime Brain Teasers

In which two songs did the Beatles sing, "She loves you, yeah, yeah, yeah"?

Answer _____

Dice Man

Using three of the arithmetical signs

+, -, x and ÷,

can you achieve the correct total?

[2] [6] [3] [5] = [3]

Top Ten

Commute Clothes:

- Overcoat ☐
- Jacket ☐
- Poncho ☐
- Cloak ☐
- Parka ☐
- Raincoat ☐
- Wind breaker ☐
- Fur coat ☐
- Anorak ☐
- Cape ☐

Guess the Phobia

Could happen on a team building course:

Anthropophobia

Work Space

The first millennium, 1-1000 AD, consisted of 365,250 days. The last millennium, 1001-2000 AD, consisted of 365,237 days. The current millennium, 2001-3000 AD, will consist of 365,242 days. The reason for the differences is the calendar system that was in use for each millennium.

Morning Meditation

There's more to the truth than just the facts.

Author Unknown

In the Calendar

In what year did Martin Luther launch the Reformation marking the start of Protestant Christianity?

Answers from previous page

Clock Watching: Answer = 6pm

Wordwheel nine-letter word: Interview

Brain Teaser: Answer = *She Loves You* and *All You Need Is Love*

Design Your Own

Unlikely Candidate

Ballerina

_____

The Word Calculator

Find the alternative words that make this sum work:

$$+ \quad \begin{array}{c} \text{ON BEHALF OF} \\ \text{MELODY} \end{array}$$

$$= \quad \text{WEALTH}$$

1	2	3	0	+
4	5	6	%	-
7	8	9	÷	=

Whatever You Do

Don't even think about any of the following...

Your appraisal meeting

Your redundancy notice

Your necessary explanation

Get the Job

Unscramble the anagram below to find the job.

Jumble Rack

Answer _____

Before they were famous

What did *Lord of the Rings* actor Orlando Bloom do before he was a famous movie star?

Extinct Jobs

Navvie:

The term "navvie" was first used as a job title for the men who dug Britain's canals, and was short for "navigator". It later became extended to include those who built the railways as well.

Answers from previous page

In the Calendar: Answer = 1517

Guess the Phobia: Answer = Fear of people

Dice Man: Answer = $3 \times 6 - 3 \div 5 = 3$

Payday for Pessimists

You've been working overtime and got a nice bit of extra pay, but last week one person who did the same died of a heart attack.

Sing While You Work...

Which song about work do the lyrics below come from?

All the rum, I want to drink it, all the whiskey too
My woman need a new dress, my daughter got to go to school

Domino Logic

Can you work out the missing number and the reason why?

Change the Word

In five steps...

Ball
___
___
___
___
Goal

Clock Watching

You start work at 8:50 a.m. For every 105 minutes work, you get a 10 minute break. How long will it be from your last break to the end of the day at 5:30 p.m?

👁 Caught by the Boss

Talking to yourself again ☐

Talking to the pot plants on your desk ☐

Not talking to anyone all day ☐

Answers from previous page

Word Calculator: Answer = (On behalf of)
For + (Melody) Tune = (Wealth) Fortune

Get the Job: Answer = Lumberjack

Before They Were Famous: Orlando Bloom worked as a clay trapper at a local pigeon shooting range when he was 13.

WORDWHEEL

Using only the letters in the Wordwheel, you have ten minutes to find as many words as possible, none of which may be plurals, foreign words or proper nouns. Each word must be of three letters or more, all must contain the central letter and letters can only be used once in every word.
There is at least one nine-letter word in the wheel.

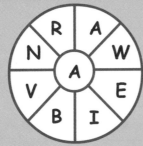

Nine-letter word _____

Word Fits

Complete these words using three four letter words. In each group of three, the missing word is the same.

FL - - -   S - - - K
H - - -   - - - D E R
C R - - -   M A - - - G
- - - E N   - - - E

Dice Man

Using three of the arithmetical signs
+, -, x and ÷,
can you achieve the correct total?

Payday for Pessimists

Yes you've been paid but they've deducted money for the days that you were late.

Clock Watching

At 1:00 p.m. you get a one-hour lunch break and the afternoon break starts 100 minutes after lunch ends. How many hours and minutes from now until the afternoon break?

Lunchtime Sudoku

	8		4		9		7	
	4			8	5	1		3
	5	2				6		
2		4		5	3			
7			6		4			9
			9	1		8		4
		1				2	3	
3		9	1	7			8	
	7		3		2		6	

Get the Job

Can you unscramble the anagram below to get the job title?

Its Pain

Answer _____

Pick 'n' Mix

Choose 3 words to describe your last desk drawer:

Messy   Rubbish

Dirty   Empty

Chaotic   Pitiful

Tidy   Awful

Organised Broken

Answers from previous page

Wordwheel nine-letter word: Brainwave

Word Fits: Answer = *Ash, Tin*

Top Ten

Tonight's TV:

- Drama ☐
- Soap opera ☐
- Documentary ☐
- News ☐
- Music ☐
- Game show ☐
- Chat show ☐
- Talent show ☐
- Reality TV ☐
- Film ☐

Board Meeting Doodle

Timewasters Synonymous

Find the missing word, which is closely related to the words on either side.

Then take the third letter of each word to make a new word.

Match *** Healthy

Stoop *** Curve

Court *** Persuade

Whatever You Do

Don't even think about any of the following:

Open healing sores

Dripping taps when you're in bed

Crushed bones beneath a bus

Place Your Bets

Your cat disappeared because:

It didn't like you	—/—
Someone stole it	—/—
Next door's dog ate it	—/—

Answers from previous page

Named and Shamed

Drunk _____

Dazed _____

Devious _____

Get the Job: Answer = Pianist

Dice Man:
Answer = 5 - 3 + 4 ÷ 1 = 6

Clock Watching:
Answer = 4 hours 25 minutes

Lunchtime Sudoku:

1	8	3	4	6	9	5	7	2
6	4	7	2	8	5	1	9	3
9	5	2	7	3	1	6	4	8
2	9	4	8	5	3	7	1	6
7	1	8	6	2	4	3	5	9
5	3	6	9	1	7	8	2	4
4	6	1	5	9	8	2	3	7
3	2	9	1	7	6	4	8	5
8	7	5	3	4	2	9	6	1

Ways to Pass the Time

Gossiping ☐

Gallivanting ☐

Gambling ☐

Design Your Own

Computer wallpaper

The Word Calculator

Find the alternative words that make this sum work:

$$\begin{array}{r} \text{SMACK} \\ + \quad \text{RUSH} \\ \hline = \quad \text{CARELESS} \end{array}$$

```
1 2 3 0 +
4 5 6 % -
7 8 9 : =
```

Brain Teaser

Which country was the first to develop ocean-going vessels during the 15th Century?

Trick Talk Detector

Your boss announces that he wants the latest product to be "leading edge."

What does he really mean?

A. A completely alien product that has no value as yet.

B. Something that will astound the world.

C. You have absolutely no idea.

Two-Word Horoscopes

Aries - Bread basket

Taurus - Insane asylum

Gemini - Hospital food

Cancer - It's broken

Leo - Know it

Virgo - Destroy it

Libra - We hear

Scorpio - Black thoughts

Sagittarius - Lovely weather

Capricorn - Please remember

Aquarius - Boring meeting

Pisces - Past it

Answers from previous page

Timewasters Synonymous: Answer = Two
(Fit, Bow, Woo)

Who Am I?

Which singer's name is hidden in the anagram below?

Join Hackle Scam

Work Face

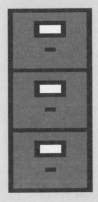

Frustrated

The Filing Cabinet

Which is the odd word out?

LULLILOO

MAMMOGRAM

REFRIGERATOR

SWALLOWWORT

WHIPPERSNAPPER

Words to Impress Your Colleagues

Test yourself and expand your vocabulary
Do you know the meaning of the word?:

Quat?

Sing While You Work

These lyrics are from a song about work.
Can you guess the song?

Nothing comes easy
But a broken back

Today's Target

To try to get through the whole day without saying hello to anyone

Brief Survival Guide

Dressing for Success:
Put your underwear on first
Try to make sure that your outfit matches
Try to make sure that your outfit fits

Mass Hysterias

Today we are all going to:
Buy only fruit grown by monks in the mountains and drink medieval ale

Answers to previous page

Brain Teaser: Answer = Portugal
The Word Calculator: Answer = (Smack) Slap + (Rush) Dash = (Careless) Slapdash

Timewasters Synonymous

Find the missing word, which is closely related to the words on either side.
Then take the first letter of each word to make a new word.

Rent *** Allow
Painting *** Skill
Understand *** Obtain

Unlikely Candidate

Chairman of the Board

_____

Around the Water Cooler

Overtime without pay ▮

Weekends without pay ▮

Next month without pay ▮

Work Space

The brightest star in the sky is Sirius. Also known as The Dog Star, it is 51 trillion miles from Earth or about 8.7 light years.

In the Calendar

What happened on March 30, 1981?

Top Five

Best songs for having an argument:

1. _____
2. _____
3. _____
4. _____
5. _____

Answers from previous page

The Filing Cabinet: Answer = Swallowwort
(the others contain a letter that repeats 4 times)

Who Am I? Answer = Michael Jackson

Words to Impress Your Colleagues: Quat refers to an insignificant person

Sing While You Work: Answer = *Work Hard* Depeche Mode

Domino Logic

Can you work out the missing number and the reason why?

 = 14

= 18

= 6

= ?

Cord to Then in 5 steps:

Cord

_____

_____

_____

_____

_____

Then

Guess the Phobia

Coffee, tea, juice, water...?

Decidophobia

Clock Watching

You are half way through the working day. In an hour and a half you will be two thirds of the way through. When will the day end?

Brief Survival Guide

Presentations:

Consider color

Wave your arms about a lot as you talk to distract people

Don't listen to criticism-they're just being spiteful

Answers from previous page

In the Calendar: Answer = President Reagan was shot and injured

Timewasters Snonymous: Answer = Lag
(Let, Art, Get)

Payday for Optimists

They won't give you overtime pay but perhaps one day your boss will stick around to see you working late.

Morning Meditation

When the student is ready, the master appears.

Buddhist Proverb

Design Your Own

Barbed wire fence:

Guess the Real Word

Galligonscious ☐

Galligodectian ☐

Galligaskins ☐

Change the Word

In 5 steps:

Deaf

_____

_____

_____

_____

Soon

Place Your Bets

_____'s tie today will be:

Multicolored, crazy-patterned   —/—

Possibly pink or yellow   —/—

A lovely velvet bow   —/—

Named and Shamed

Least trustworthy   _____

Least likeable   _____

Least loveable   _____

Unlikely Candidate

Career Criminal   _____

Mass Hysterias	Mind Games
Today we are all going to: Wear matching dresses, shake bells and dance in the street	Boss says: "I can't do this all by myself." Boss means: "I have far too many business lunches and dinners to attend to."

Answers from previous page

Change the Word: Answer = Cord, Corn, Coin, Chin, Thin, Then

Clock Watching: Answer = 6 O'clock

Guess the Phobia: Answer = Fear of making decisions

Domino Logic: Answer = 18
(subtract the sixth number from the sum of the first five)

The Filing Cabinet

Which is the odd word out?

CICADELLIDAE
GRADGRINDIAN
HAPPENCHANCE
PANAMANIAN
TRISECTRICES

Work Face

One hour to go

Unlikely Candidate

Teacher of the Year

_____

Whatever You Do

Don't even think about any of the following:

Scrtaching noises in the night

Squelching noises underfoot

Screeches from the tree tops

Guess the Real Word

Which is the real word?

Lollygotious   ☐

Liripipe   ☐

Lollynoxious   ☐

Get the Job

Unscramble the anagram below to find the job.

TEETH AL

Answer _____

Before They Were Famous

Boy George is known for his music, his make-up and his outrageous clothes. What was his job before he became famous?

Answer _____

Answers from previous page:

Change Word: Deaf,Leaf,Loaf, Loan,Loon,Soon

Real Word: Answer = Galligaskins (Wide, very loose breeches.)

Domino Logic

What is the missing number?

= 5

= 4

= 6

= ?

Breaktime Brain Teasers

The 13th-century travel book called *The Million* describes the travels of which famous sailor?

Which Movie Contains the Following Quote?

"Work, work, work. Work, work, work. Work, work, work. Hello boys, have a good night's rest, I missed you."

Today's Target

To take a three hour lunch break and see if anyone notices

Top Ten

Ambient Lighting:

Candles ☐
Lamps ☐
Strip lighting ☐
Torch ☐
Gas lamp ☐
Oil lamp ☐
Tea light ☐
Chandelier ☐
Ceiling light ☐
Wall light ☐

Sing While You Work

Which song about work contains the following words?

Fold my hands and pray for rain, I got a head full of ideas.

Answers from previous page

Real Word: Answer = Liripipe (a part or lesson committed to memory.)
Get the Job: Answer = Athlete
Before They Were Famous:
Answer = Boy George worked in a supermarket
The Filing Cabinet: Answer = Panamanian (in the others, each letter in the word occurs twice)

Wordwheel

Using only the letters in the wordwheel, you have ten minutes to find as many words as possible, none of which may be plurals, foreign words or proper nouns. Each word must be of three letters or more, all must contain the central letter and letters can only be used once in every word.
There is at least one nine-letter word in the wheel.

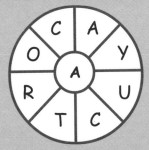

Nine-letter word _____

Excuses for...

Going barefoot:

_____
_____
_____

Work Face

Aggressive email

Word Fits

Complete these words using two three-letter words. In each group of four, the missing word is the same.

- - - E   C O - - -
- - - T E S T   - - - I E R
S - - - E   - - - A L
- - - I F E R   - - - H A N E

Thought for the Day

"Being a good artist is the toughest job you could pick, and you have to be a little nuts to take it on. I love them all."
Charles Saatchi

Answers from previous page

Sing While You Work: Answer = *Maggie's Farm*
Bob Dylan

Movie Quote = *Blazing Saddles* (1974)

Brain Teaser: Answer = Marco Polo

Domino Logic: Answer = 6
(the sum of the spots of each domino in the row)

Find the Muffin

The first player brings a treat into the office: a muffin, cake, chocolate bar or other sugar-based piece of joy. For the sake of the instructions, we will assume this to be a chocolate muffin. They place this treat into a plain cardboard box and write the name of the contents on the side (eg CHOCOLATE MUFFIN).

They then hide this treat somewhere in plain view around the office (for instance the shelf over the radiator, in the night manager's pigeonhole or on top of the contracts filing cabinet.

The players are given a signal that it is time to start the hunt. They then leave their desks and circulate around the office trying to spot the muffin. It is important that non-players should not realize what the game is, so the hunters should attempt to look as though they are involved in important work-related tasks.

Winner gets to eat the muffin. Then next day they become the first player, who chooses and hides the treat.

Dice Man

Using three of the arithmetical signs $+$, $-$, $\times$ and $\div$, can you achieve the correct total?

Payday for Pessimists

It's pay day but you've been made redundant.

Get the Job

Can you unscramble the anagram to reveal the job title?

Gloomiest Rote

Answer _____

Pick 'n' Mix

Choose 3 words to describe your colleagues:

Idiots	Trendy
Mates	Nerds
Spiteful	Laughable
Malicious	Cool
Caring	Supportive

Answers from previous page

Word Fits: Answer = Con, Met

Wordwheel nine-letter word: Autocracy

Timewasters Synonymous

Find the missing word, which is closely related to the words on either side.

Then take the second letter of each word to make a new word.

Leak *** Slop**
Coin ** Herb**
Encounter ** Gather**

Today's Greatest Achievement

Eating three pies ☐
Energy in bundles ☐
Spontaneity at every moment ☐

Which Movie Contains the Following Quote?

"I realize that I'm the president of this company, the man that's responsible for everything that goes on here. So, I want to state, right now, that anything that happened is not my fault."

Work Face

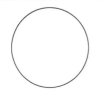

Colleague with body odor

Top Five

Best songs for lunch at your desk:
1. _____
2. _____
3. _____
4. _____
5. _____

Breaktime Brain Teasers

What was ther name of the British politician who was suceeded as Prime Minister by Winston Churchill in 1940?

Mind Games

Boss says: "I'm going out and I'll be unreachable for the rest of the afternoon."
Boss means: "I'm off to get very drunk."

Unlikely Candidate

Pin-up model

_____

Answers from previous page

Get the Job: Answer = Meteorologist

Dice Man: Answer = 4 + 6 - 5 ÷ 5 = 1

Lasso Hullaballoo

This can be a solo game, or a contest between co-workers.

First construct a lasso out of elastic bands.

Secondly, choose an object on your desk and attempt to lasso it and pull it towards you. A pen tray, coffee mug or stapler will make a suitable target.

When successful, you may like to shout "Yee-hah" at the top of your voice. When unsuccessful, the appropriate phrase is "Well, I'll be danged."

Repeat the game until physically restrained from doing so by colleagues.

Place Your Bets

_____ 's desk drawer is:

Obssessively neat   —/—

Abysmally untidy   —/—

Disgustingly dirty   —/—

The Filing Cabinet

Which is the odd word out?

HOTSHOTS

NATIONALIZATION

NEANDERTHAL

PATINATING

UNDERGROUNDER

Brief Survival Guide

Starting a New Job:

Aim to get there on the specified day

Try to remember what you are supposed to be doing

Don't wear sequins or feathers (unless you are required to)

Answers from previous page

Timewasters Synonymous: Answer = Pie (Spill, Mint, Meet)

Movie Quote: Answer = *How to Succeed in Business Without Really Trying* (1967)

Brain Teaser: Answer = Neville Chamberlain

Trick Talk Detector

Your boss announces that he wants you to "front end" a piece of work.

What does he really mean?

A: He wants you to ram it with bulldozer.

B: He wants you to turn it back to front.

C: He wants you to concentrate on this
   and only this.

Answer: Smash it.

Ways to Pass the Time

Tripping ☐

Trotting ☐

Telling ☐

Design Your Own

Trendy haircut:

Word Fits

Complete these words using two three-letter words. In each group of four, the missing word is the same.

```
        S - - -E
        - - -I F U L
        C A - - -U L A T E

W H - - -A S      - - -G E N T
T H - - -         D I S - - -T
H - - -I N        S - - -D
```

Today's Greatest Achievement

No headaches ☐

Cleaned the bathroom ☐

Not having an argument

In the Calendar

What happened on April 26, 1986?

Answers from previous page

The Filing Cabinet: Answer = Neanderthal (the others contain repeating sequences of letters: ation, under, atin, hots)

The Word Calculator

Find the alternative words that make this sum work:

BOAT

+

FORM

─────────

= ORDERLY

```
1 2 3 0 +
4 5 6 % -
7 8 9 ÷ =
```

Who Am I?

Can you work out which singer's name is hidden in the anagram below?

IT'S NASAL, TIRESOME

Work Face

Overheard

Words to Impress Your Colleagues

Test yourself and expand your vocabulary.
Do you know the meaning of the word:

Pronk?

My Next Sick Day

What _____

When _____

How _____

Today's Target

To shout "YES SIR" each time you're asked to do something no matter who asks

Brief Survival Guide

Job Interview:

1. Medication

2. Knowledge

3. Stay at home

Mass Hysterias

Today we are all going to...
Climb to the top of a tall tree and stay there fasting for the next year

Answers from previous page

Word Fits: Answer = Pit, Ere, Tan

In the Calendar: Answer = Nuclear disaster at Chernobyl

Wordwheel

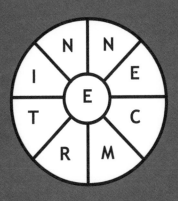

Using only the letters in the Wordwheel, you have ten minutes to find as many words as possible, none of which may be plurals, foreign words or proper nouns. Each word must be of three letters or more, all must contain the central letter and letters can only be used once in every word. There is at least one nine-letter word in the wheel.

Nine-letter word: _____

Ridiculous Rules

In Kentucky you are apparently deemed "sober" as long as you can hold on to the ground.

Breaktime Brain Teasers

He was nicknamed the "Desert Fox" but what was the real name of Hitler's most prominent field marshal?

Answer _____

Clock Watching

Lunchtime is at 12:25
How long to wait?

Work Space

The largest asteroid on record is *Ceres*. It is so big it would stretch from Washington D.C. to Louisville, Kentucky (600 miles).

Dice Man

Using three of the arithmetical signs
+, -, x and ÷,
can you achieve the correct total?

Top Ten

Home-Sweet-Home:

House	☐
Apartment	☐
Hotel	☐
Cabin	☐
Trailer	☐
Tent	☐
Beach house	☐
Penthouse	☐
Tenement	☐
Mansion	☐

Guess the Phobia

When you feel challenged in the vocabulary department:

Sesquipedalophobia

Guess the Real Word?

Funogometry ☐

Funototality ☐

Famulus ☐

Morning Meditation

Only that in you which is me can hear what I'm saying

Baba Ram Dass

In the Calendar

In what year was Buddha, founder of Budhism born?

Answers from previous page

Clock Watching: Answer = 4 hours 45 minutes

Wordwheel nine-letter word: Increment

Brain Teaser: Answer = Erwin Rommel

Design Your Own

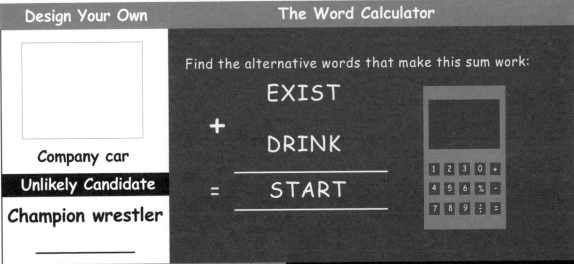

[blank box]

Company car

Unlikely Candidate

Champion wrestler

_____

The Word Calculator

Find the alternative words that make this sum work:

EXIST

+

DRINK
_____

= START
_____

Whatever You Do

Don't even think about any of the following:

Police at your door in the dark

Rabid Dogs at your door in the dark

Your heating bill on a cold, dark day

Get the Job

Unscramble the anagram below to find the job.

Motorcar Germ Pumper

Answer _____

Before They Were Famous

Robin Williams is famous for his high-energy acting performances on screen and on stage. However, what job did he have before he was famous?

Pick 'n' Mix

Delete as appropriate:

Last weekend was fun/boring/crazy. My mother-in-law/bestfriend/neighbour came over and we had a huge fight/party/discussion because I had won/lost/broken their favorite ring/potato chips/car.

Answers from previous page

In the Calendar: Answer = 486 BC

Guess the Phobia: Answer = Fear of long words

Dice Man: Answer = 2 x 3 + 4 - 5 = 5

Real Word: Famulus refers to a private secretary or attendant.

Payday for Optimists

Money, money, money. So what if you haven't slept more than 3 hours a night all week?

Sing While You Work...

Which song about work do the lyrics below come from?

But I've got the power, and I've got the will
I'm not a charity case

Domino Logic

Can you work out the missing number and the reason why?

= 14

= 24

= 99

= ?

Change the Word

In seven steps...

Busy

———

———

———

———

———

Lazy

Today's Target

Tap dance on the desk every time the clock strikes the hour

Clock Watching

Coffee break is at 11:05. How long to wait?

Caught by the Boss

Last in the door ☐

First out the door ☐

First to the drinks area ☐

WORDWHEEL

Using only the letters in the Wordwheel, you have ten minutes to find as many words as possible, none of which may be plurals, foreign words or proper nouns. Each word must be of three letters or more, all must contain the central letter and letters can only be used once in every word.
There is at least one nine-letter word in the wheel.

Nine-letter word _____

Word Fits

Complete these words using three three-letter words. In each group of three, the missing word is the same.

H - - -
IMP - - - D
T - - - NT   S - - - N
                - - - L
                S - - - P

- - - T E R
T O I - - -
- - - T I N G

Today's Target

To organize everything on your desk in alphabetical order

Thought For the Day

In the end, we will remember not the words of our enemies, but the silence of our friends.

Martin Luther King, Jr.

Answers from previous page

Domino Logic: Answer = 12 (multiply all the left hand sides together and all the right hand sides, subtract the latter from the former)

Clock Watching: Answer = 2 hours 45 minutes

Change the Word:
busy, bush, lush, lash, lakh, laky, lazy

Sing While You Work: Answer = *Blue Collar Man* Styx

Dice Man

Using three of the arithmetical signs
+, -, x and ÷,
can you achieve the correct total?

Payday for Pessimists

You have asked your boss for a pay raise for the last two years but he always says no.

Word Fits

Complete these words using three three-letter words. In each group of three, the missing word is the same.

S H - - -
F - - - I G N
M - - -

S P - - -
- - - Y
C - - - E D

S T I F - - -
- - - E R
B A R - - -

Lunchtime Sudoku

			9	2	3			
6		7						9
2	4			7		8	1	
3	6	4	7			1		
7			2		4			9
		8			1	5	7	4
	9	3		1			8	2
	1					6		7
			4	5	2			

Get the Job

Can you unscramble the anagram below to get the job title?

Name Chic

Answer _____

Pick 'n' Mix

Choose 3 words to describe your schooldays:

Pointless   Educational

Enjoyable   Boring

Useless   Brilliant

Painful   Brutal

Torturous   Purposeful

Answers from previous page

Wordwheel nine-letter word: Swindling

Word Fits: Answer = Ale, Woo, Let

Top Ten

Bar Room Sports Discussion:

- Football ☐
- Baseball ☐
- Tennis ☐
- Hockey ☐
- Soccer ☐
- Swimming ☐
- Track ☐
- Horse racing ☐
- Wrestling ☐
- Boxing ☐

Board Meeting Doodle

Place Your Bets

_____'s going out outfit will be:

Multicolored, eccentric and dizzying —/—

Probably boring and bland —/—

Just plain weird and scary —/—

Named and Shamed

Biggest ego _____

Biggest fantasist _____

Biggest beer goggles _____

Timewasters Synonymous

Find the missing word, which is closely related to the words on either side.

Then take the fourth letter of each word to make a new word.

Boundary **** Adjoin**

Alcohol **** Soul**

Dairy **** Schmaltz**

Insult **** Partial**

Whatever You Do

Don't even think about any of the following:

Your upcoming presentation

Your useless time-keeping

Your total inability to work

Answers from previous page

Get the Job:
Answer = Mechanic

Dice Man:
Answer = 3 + 4 - 2 x 1 = 5

Word Fits:
Answer = Ore, Oil, Fly

Lunchtime Sudoku:

1	8	5	9	2	3	7	4	6
6	3	7	1	4	8	2	9	5
2	4	9	5	7	6	8	1	3
3	6	4	7	9	5	1	2	8
7	5	1	2	8	4	3	6	9
9	2	8	3	6	1	5	7	4
5	9	3	6	1	7	4	8	2
4	1	2	8	3	9	6	5	7
8	7	6	4	5	2	9	3	1

Ways to Pass the Time

Stealing ☐

Chasing ☐

Accosting ☐

Design Your Own

Golf sweater

The Word Calculator

Find the alternative words that make this sum work:

$$\begin{array}{r} \text{NEGATION} \\ + \quad \text{ENTITY} \\ \hline = \quad \text{ZERO} \end{array}$$

Brain Teaser

What was the name of the legendary Russian sniper of the Battle of Stalingrad, fictionalized in the film, *Enemy at the Gates*?

Trick Talk Detector

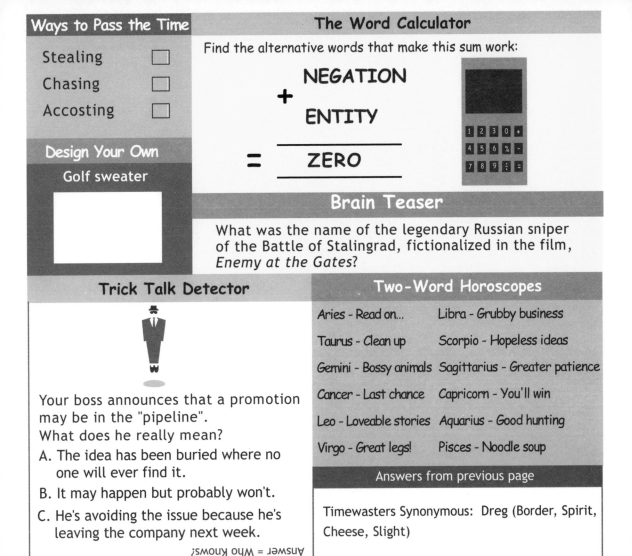

Your boss announces that a promotion may be in the "pipeline".
What does he really mean?

A. The idea has been buried where no one will ever find it.

B. It may happen but probably won't.

C. He's avoiding the issue because he's leaving the company next week.

Answer = Who Knows?

Two-Word Horoscopes

Aries - Read on...   Libra - Grubby business

Taurus - Clean up   Scorpio - Hopeless ideas

Gemini - Bossy animals   Sagittarius - Greater patience

Cancer - Last chance   Capricorn - You'll win

Leo - Loveable stories   Aquarius - Good hunting

Virgo - Great legs!   Pisces - Noodle soup

Answers from previous page

Timewasters Synonymous: Dreg (Border, Spirit, Cheese, Slight)

Who Am I?

Which singer's name is hidden in the anagram below?

Er, Doesn't View

Work Face

Overtired

The Filing Cabinet

Which is the odd word out?

AARDVARK

EEL

EASEL

LLAMA

OODLES

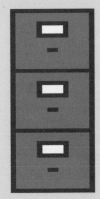

Words to Impress Your Colleagues

Test yourself and expand your vocabulary
Do you know the meaning of the word:

Abessive?

Sing While You Work

These lyrics are from a song about work.
Can you guess the song?

Take your instinct by the reins
Your better best to rearrange

Today's Target

To disguise yourself whenever you leave the office so the receptionist doesn't recognize you

Brief Survival Guide

Resignation:
Put a password lock on all your computer files.
Put some rotting food in your desk drawer.
Tell everyone exactly what you think of them and then run.

Mass Hysterias

Today we are all going to:
Go outside and stamp our feet in unison as a warning to anybody who tries to subdue us.

Answers to previous page

Brain Teaser: Answer = Vasily Zaytsev
The Word Calculator: Answer = (Negation) No + (Entity) Thing = Nothing

Timewasters Synonymous

Find the missing word, which is closely related to the words on either side.
Then take the last letter of each word to make a new word.

Angry ***** Intersect
Near ***** Shut
Scarf ***** Robbed
Educate ***** Locomotive

Unlikely Candidate

Chief cleaner

_____

Around the Water Cooler

New supervisor on the way ▮

New receptionist on the way ▮

New job on the way ▮

Work Space

The first time humans left Earth was on December 21, 1968. Apollo 8 was the first manned space vehicle to leave Earth's orbit and to orbit the Moon.

In the Calendar

What happened on January 22, 1901?

Top Five

Best songs for getting ready for work:
1. _____
2. _____
3. _____
4. _____
5. _____

Answers from previous page

The Filing Cabinet: Answer = Easel (the others start with a repeated letter)

Who Am I? Answer = Stevie Wonder

Words: Abessive means indicating absence or lack

Sing While You Work: Answer = *Finest Worksong* R.E.M

Domino Logic

Can you work out the missing number and the reason why?

⚅	⚄	⚅	= 1
⚅	⚄	⚅	= 3
⚅	⚅	⚅	= 1
⚅	⚅	⚅	= ?

Change the Word

In 5 steps:

Boss

_____

_____

_____

_____

_____

Sane

Guess the Phobia

Your boss suggests you go on a course:

Sophophobia

Clock Watching

Your working hours are 11:00 a.m. to 7:00 p.m. You are closer to the start than the end of the working day. Is it the afternoon or the middle of the night?

Brief Survival Guide

Over-enthusiastic assistant:

Freeze them out

Speak only in an undetectable foreign language

Just growl whenever they get too close

Answers from previous page

In the Calendar: Answer = Queen Victoria died in England

Timewasters Synonymous: Answer = Seen (Cross, Close, Stole, Train)

Payday for Optimists

It's snowing outside but you can almost afford some thick, woolly socks and good boots now.

Morning Meditation

You can't reason someone out of a position they didn't reason themselves into.

Author Unknown

Design Your Own

Baseball stadium:

Guess the Real Word

Gongoozler ☐

Gongozeniar ☐

Gongenococity ☐

Change the Word

In 4 steps:

Warm

_____

_____

_____

_____

Cold

Place Your Bets

This morning's meeting will be:

Lively, fun and inspirational —/—

Dull, dreary and pointless —/—

Terrifying, troublesome and difficult —/—

Named and Shamed

Diva _____

Desperate _____

Dreary _____

Unlikely Candidate

Womanizer _____

Mass Hysterias

Today we are all going to:

Cut the nails on our left hand very short and grow the nails on our right very long.

Mind Games

Boss says: "My door is always open if you ever need to discuss it with me."

Boss means: "Shut up."

Answers from previous page

Change the Word: Answer = boss, bass, sass, sans sane

Clock Watching: Answer = The middle of the night

Guess the Phobia: Answer = Fear of learning

Domino Logic: Answer = 2 (divide the sum of the left hand sides by the sum of the right hand sides)

The Filing Cabinet

Which is the odd word out?

ASTEROID
JUPITER
MERCURY
METEOR
MYRTLE

Work Face

Office crush

Unlikely Candidate

Best in show

_____

Whatever You Do

Don't even think about any of the following:

The smell of hospital food

The sound of the dentist's drill

Rats chewing the phone line

Guess the Real Word

Which is the real word?

Octonocity ☐

Orphrey ☐

Octobucculus ☐

Get the Job

Unscramble the anagram below to find the job.

COY KEJ

Answer _____

Before They Were Famous

Danny DeVito is now a major movie star but what did he do before he was famous?

Answer _____

Answers from previous page:

Change the Word: Warm, Ward, Card, Cord, Cold

Real Word = Gongoozler (An idle spectator)

Domino Logic: Answer = 2

Domino Logic

What is the missing number?

= 2

= 5

= 2

= ?

Breaktime Brain Teasers

How many years in prison did the twelve members of the Great Train Robbery gang get between them in 1964?

Which Movie Contains the Following Quote?

" If I'm working late, you gotta work late! If you can't work late, I can't work late! If I can't work late, I can't work late!"

Today's Target

To ask "How?" every time you're asked to do something

Top Ten

Desk decoration:

Photos ☐
Paper weight ☐
Diary ☐
Pot plant ☐
Fruit bowl ☐
Pen holder ☐
Stapler ☐
Flowers ☐
Lamp ☐
Music player ☐

Sing While You Work

Which song about work contains the following words?

Brush up on my field work
Better brush up on my field work
Gonna get my fingers dirty

Answers from previous page

Real Word: Answer = Orphrey (Gold or other rich embroidery)
Get the Job: Answer = Jockey
Before They Were Famous:
Answer = Danny de Vito used to be a hairstylist
The Filing Cabinet: Answer = Myrtle (the others are astronomical objects)

Wordwheel

Using only the letters in the wordwheel, you have ten minutes to find as many words as possible, none of which may be plurals, foreign words or proper nouns. Each word must be of three letters or more, all must contain the central letter and letters can only be used once in every word.

There is at least one nine-letter word in the wheel.

Nine-letter word _____

Excuses for...

A loud scream:

_____

_____

_____

Work Face

Bad back

Word Fits

Complete these words using three three-letter words. In each group of three, the missing word is the same.

S - - - N E R

- - - T

D E S - - - T

    F R O N - - - R

    - - - R

    U N - - - D

G O L - - -

- - - T E D

S U D - - -

Thought for the Day

Do not say a little in many words but a great deal in a few.

Pythagoras

The Long Walk

Many of the most self-important people in the workplace like to walk very quickly around the office in order to convey the idea that they are too stressed, overloaded or significant to pause for thought or chat to lesser mortals.

In this game the challenge is to invert this attitude by walking as slowly as possible around the office for a day.

How slowly can you walk from your desk to the water cooler and back again without anyone realizing that you are doing it on purpose?

Smile, chat, look out of the window at the blue sky beyond. Make it as clear as possible that you are not busy, have nothing better to do, and are not above conversing with your fellow workers.

When you eventually get back to your desk, award yourself points based on your performance.

Dice Man

Using three of the arithmetical signs $+, -, \times$ and $\div$, can you achieve the correct total?

Payday for Pessimists

Another pay day, another hangover

Get the Job

Can you unscramble the anagram to reveal the job title?

I Ran Me

Answer _____

Pick 'n' Mix

Choose 3 words to describe your office dress sense:

Criminal   Tarty

Trendy   Inimitable

Cool   Suspicious

Ridiculous   Stylish

Casual   Tasteful

Answers from previous page

Word Fits: Answer = Can, Tie, Den

Wordwheel nine-letter word: Interview

Timewasters Synonymous

Find the missing word, which is closely related to the words on either side.

Then take the third letter of each word to make a new four-letter word.

Beak ** Demand**
Metal ** Rule**
Penalty ** Clement**
Stair ** Progress**

Today's Greatest Achievement

- A tidy desk ☐
- Saying the right things ☐
- No cigarettes ☐

Which Movie Contains the Following Quote?

" I was in the Marines, too. So what is it? You need an extra job? Are you moonlighting?"

" Well I, I just want to work long hours. What's 'moonlighting'?"

Work Face

◯

Colleague's promotion

Top Five

Best songs for writing a resignation letter:

1. _____
2. _____
3. _____
4. _____
5. _____

Breaktime Brain Teasers

This man was a historical Chinese Marxist political leader from 1949 until his death in 1976. What was his name?

Mind Games

Boss says: "This is a very sensitive issue."

Boss means: "You're going to find what I have to say upsetting."

Unlikely Candidate

Racing driver

_____

Answers from previous page

Get the Job: Answer = Marine

Dice Man: Answer = 1 + 1 x 3 ÷ 1 = 6

Finger Wrestling

This game is very similar to arm wrestling, but is played using a single finger instead of the full arm.

Contestants sit opposite each other across a desk or other table.

Each places their right (or left) hand on the table resting their wrist on the table, with one finger pointing upwards.

Each tries to push the other contestant's finger down towards the table.

The loser is the one whose finger is pushed back against the table, or taps the table in surrender first.

Place Your Bets

The new receptionist is:

Easy on the eye	—/—
Completely clueless	—/—
Possibly psychotic	—/—

The Filing Cabinet

Which is the odd word out?

AMBIDEXTROUSLY
CONSUMPTIVELY
CONCATENATION
FLAMETHROWING
UNDISCOVERABLY
UNPREDICTABLY

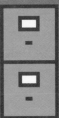

Brief Survival Guide

Writing a CV:

You know you are fabulous

Try to make it at least slightly relevant to your abilities

Don't write any obvious lies (e.g. you used to run the U.N.)

Answers from previous page

Timewasters Synonymous: Answer = Lane (bill, lead, fine, step)

Movie Quote: Answer = *Taxi Driver* (1976)

Brain Teaser: Answer = Mao Zedong

Trick Talk Detector

Your boss tells you that he thinks it is time you "put to bed" a certain project.

What does he really mean?

A: He wants you to wrap it in a blanket and put it in your desk drawer.

B: He wants you cut your losses and run.

C: He doesn't care what happens to it any more.

Answer: You can now sneak out of the office quietly.

Ways to Pass the Time

Sniffling ☐
Snoring ☐
Swindling ☐

Design Your Own

Football shirt:

Word Fits

Complete these words using two three-letter words. In each group of four, the missing word is the same.

```
- - - I S H        - - - E
- - - A L      D E S - - - Y
- - - E        S - - - K


   W O O D - - - E
   - - - D I N G
   C U R - - - G
```

Today's Greatest Achievement

A happy mind ☐
Saving your soul ☐
Cleanr head ☐

In the Calendar

What happened on October 1, 1936?

Answers from previous page

The Filing Cabinet: Answer = Concatenation (none of the others contain any repetitions of the same letter)

The Word Calculator

Find the alternative words that make this sum work:

VEHICLE

+ WEIGHT

= CONTAINER

```
1 2 3 0 +
4 5 6 % -
7 8 9 ÷ =
```

Who Am I?

Can you work out
which singer's name is hidden
in the anagram below?

METAL OAF

Work Face

Paranoid

Words to Impress Your Colleagues

Test yourself and expand your vocabulary.

Do you know the meaning of the word:

Tanti?

My Next Must Do

What _____

When _____

How _____

Today's Target

To give an angry look to anyone who says hello to you

Brief Survival Guide

Tedious meeting:
1. Improve your doodle ability
2. Don't meet anyone's eyes
3. Sing quietly to yourself

Mass Hysterias

Today we are all going to...
Put chicken wire over the windows so the monkey man can't get in

Answers from previous page

Word Fits: Answer = Fin, Bin, Tin

In the Calendar: Answer = General Francisco Franco became leader of the Nationalist government in Spain.

Wordwheel

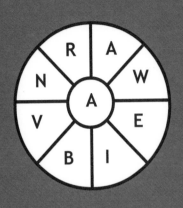

Using only the letters in the Wordwheel, you have ten minutes to find as many words as possible, none of which may be plurals, foreign words or proper nouns. Each word must be of three letters or more, all must contain the central letter and letters can only be used once in every word. There is at least one nine-letter word in the wheel.

Nine-letter word: _____

Ridiculous Rules

In the UK city of York, it is legal to murder a Scotsman within the ancient city walls, but only if he is carrying a bow and arrow.

Clock Watching

Your afternoon break is at 3:30. How long to wait?

Work Space

Any free-moving liquid in outer space will form itself into a sphere, because of its surface tension.

Breaktime Brain Teasers

How many centuries did The Age of Exploration span?

Answer _____

Answers from previous page

The Word Calculator: Answer = (Vehicle) Car + (Weight) Ton = (Container) Carton

Who Am I? Answer = Meat Loaf

Impress Your Colleagues: Answer = Tanti means something is worthwhile

Dice Man

Using three of the arithmetical signs

+, -, × and ÷,

can you achieve the correct total?

[dice] [dice] [dice] [dice] = [dice]

Top Ten

Work footwear:

- Loafers ☐
- Riding boots ☐
- Dr Martens ☐
- Espadrilles ☐
- High heel pumps ☐
- Flat sandals ☐
- Suede shoes ☐
- Jazz shoes ☐
- Snow shoes ☐
- Sneakers ☐

Guess the Phobia

When the boss invites you into his office:

Kathisophobia

Guess the Real Word

Phrontistery ☐

Pecksnicious ☐

Pecksnipperty ☐

Morning Meditation

It takes all the running you can do just to keep in the same place.

Lewis Carroll

In the Calendar

In what year did the foundation of Rome occur?

Answers from previous page

Clock Watching: Answer = 1 hour 35 minutes

Wordwheel nine-letter word: Answer = Brainwave

Brain Teaser: Answer = 4 (15th to 19th centuries)

Design Your Own

[Reception space]

Reception space

Unlikely Candidate

Mr. Universe

_____

The Word Calculator

Find the alternative words that make this sum work:

CONSUME

+

FEWER

_____

= WORTHLESS

Whatever You Do

Don't even think about any of the following:

Your computer losing all your files

Your boss reading your private emails

Your mother meeting the management

Get the Job

Unscramble the anagram below to find the job.

Bread Rent

Answer _____

Before They Were Famous

Actor Brad Pitt is known for his movie star good looks but he didn't start out that way. What did he do before he was famous?

Pick 'n' Mix

Delete as appropriate:

My sister is a lunatic/lawyer/lazy girl. Last week she asked me to go with her to the movies/mall/doctor because she had stolen/lost/broken an old jar of pickles under her jeans/shirt/hat and wanted it surgically removed/mended/cosmetically enhanced.

Answers from previous page

In the Calendar: Answer = 753 BC
Guess the Phobia: Answer = Fear of sitting down
Real Word: Answer = Phrontistery (A thinking-place; a place for study)
Dice Man: Answer = 3 x 6 - 3 ÷ 5 = 3

Payday for Optimists

Great! Your bank account is in the black and you can begin to save for a down payment for a house without a leaky roof and damp walls.

Sing While You Work...

Which song about work do the lyrics below come from?

People, go against the grain,
with their greed.
I've been here before,
it ain't gonna work no more.

Domino Logic

Can you work out the missing number and the reason why?

= 15

= 9

= 2

= ?

Change the Word

In four steps...

Fold

_____

_____

_____

_____

Soul

Today's Target

To practice yodelling everytime you go to the bathroom

Clock Watching

Your next break is at 1:10. How long to wait?

👁 Caught by the Boss

Flirting on the phone ☐

Flirting across the desk ☐

Talking to the pigeons ☐

Answers from previous page

Word Calculator: Answer = (Consume)
Use + (Fewer) Less = (Worthless) Useless

Get the Job: Answer = Bartender

Before They Were Famous: Brad Pitt was a children's entertainer dressed as a chicken.

WORDWHEEL

Using only the letters in the Wordwheel, you have ten minutes to find as many words as possible, none of which may be plurals, foreign words or proper nouns. Each word must be of three letters or more, all must contain the central letter and letters can only be used once in every word.
There is at least one nine-letter word in the wheel.

Nine-letter word _____

Word Fits

Complete these words using three three-letter words. In each group of three, the missing word is the same.

C - - - E
B - - -
M A - - - B A

    A R - - -
    I N - - -
    - - - H I C

W - - - E
- - - T I N G
- - - C H

Thought for the Day

For it isn't enough to talk about peace. One must believe in it. And it isn't enough to believe in it. One must work for it. Eleanor Roosevelt

Answers from previous page

Domino Logic: Answer = 7 (each row is a series, where the sum of each domino increases or decreases at a fixed rate)

Clock Watching: Answer = 1 hour 45 minutes

Change the Word: fold, food, fool, foul, soul

Sing While You Work: Answer = *Tape Loop* Morcheeba

Dice Man

Using three of the arithmetical signs +, -, × and ÷, can you achieve the correct total?

Payday for Pessimists

The pay is great but your boss is psychotic.

Word Fits

Complete these words using three three-letter words. In each group of three, the missing word is the same.

```
A - - - E
- - - T E R
- - - C H

- - - E D
- - - U A T E
T R A N - - -

S - - - I S H
- - - D I N G
R O - - -
```

Lunchtime Sudoku

	1	5		4		7	9	
	8			7			2	
2			3	1				5
	3	7	5		6	1	4	
1			7		8			6
	2	6	1		4	8	7	
9			6					7
	6			1			3	
	5	1		8		9	6	

Get the Job

Can you unscramble the anagram below to get the job title?

I Try Its Lash

Answer _____

Pick 'n' Mix

Delete as appropriate:

My partner/boiler/car had a breakdown/misunderstanding/rupture and just as I was dealing with that, the dog/parrot/toddler escaped.

Answers from previous page

Wordwheel nine-letter word = Autocracy

Word Fits: Answer = Rim, Got, Hit

Office Consequences

This is an email version of the original parlour game. It can be played by 2, 4, or 8 players plus a co-ordinator (who may also be a player).

The co-ordinator sends the list below to each player, asking them to fill in their share of the missing pieces of information (preferably focusing on people and places connected to the workplace).

Name One
Met (Name Two)
In/At/On (Place)
He said (What he said)
She said (What she said)
He did (What he did)
She did (What she did)
The consequences were
(What the consequences were)

The co-ordinator then sends the final version back to all players (being careful to avoid sending it as a global email, especially if any bosses have been named).

Timewasters Synonymous

Find the missing word, which is closely related to the words on either side.

Then take the third letter of each word to make a new word.

Stuff ** Pack**
Forest ** Timber**
Sleet ** Greet**
Queue ** Row**

Whatever You Do

Don't even think about any of the following:

There are burglars in your house

There are robbers in your bank

There are rats in your basement

Answers from previous page

Get the Job:
Answer = Hair Stylist

Dice Man:
Answer = 2 - 1 x 6 ÷ 1 = 6

Word Fits:
Answer = Bat, Sit, Wed

Lunchtime Sudoku:

8	1	5	8	4	2	7	9	3
4	8	3	9	7	5	6	2	1
2	7	9	3	6	1	4	8	5
8	3	7	5	9	6	1	4	2
1	9	4	7	2	8	3	5	6
5	2	6	1	3	4	8	7	9
9	4	8	6	5	3	2	1	7
7	6	2	4	1	9	5	3	8
3	5	1	2	8	7	9	6	4

Clock Watching

In an hour and a quarter, you'll be a third of the way through the shift you started 55 minutes ago. When do you finish?

The Word Calculator

Find the alternative words that make this sum work:

$$+ \begin{array}{r} \text{TAXI} \\ \text{RULED} \\ \hline \text{SENT} \end{array} =$$

Payday for Optimists

Working so hard for $5 an hour, you're bound to get a promotion soon.

Office Aviation Challenge

This game can be played in any office where there are windows above the first floor that look out onto a clear space such as a car park or landscaped garden.

Each player constructs a flying device from paper. This can be an old-fashioned paper airplane, a more elaborate version, a helicopter made from pipe cleaners or whatever else the imagination might stretch to.

Each player takes turns to launch their construction from the same window.

The winner is the player whose flying device travels the furthest.

Repeat until the amusement value starts to fade.

Answers from previous page

Timewasters Synonymous: Loin (Fill, Wood, Hail, Line)

Who Am I?

Which singer's name is hidden in the anagram below?

Voice Sells Lot

Work Face

Daydreaming

The Filing Cabinet

Which is the odd word out?

BLACKBALLED

NONSUPPORT

SOUPSPOONS

TOPSY-TURVY

ZOOSPOROUS

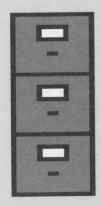

Words to Impress Your Colleagues

Test yourself and expand your vocabulary
Do you know the meaning of the word:

Hamose?

Sing While You Work

These lyrics are from a song about work.
Can you guess the song?

Come together and make it work, yeah!
We can make it work;
We can make it work.

Today's Target

To stay home as long as possible until someone tries to contact you

Brief Survival Guide

Sunday Barbecue:

Invite only colleagues you like and who like each other.

Invite all your ex's and then leave them to it.

Don't invite anyone at all.

Mass Hysterias

Today we are all going to:

Walk in the middle of the road with our eyes closed and no protective clothing

Answers to previous page

Clock Watching: Answer = 5:10
The Word Calculator: Answer = (Taxi) Cab + (Ruled) Led = (Sent) Cabled

Chatty Charades

This is one for a very slow day, where there is not enough real work to pass the time. In any office there are a certain number of things that colleagues need to communicate to one another.

The challenge is to see how long you can communicate without words.

Use finger signals to indicate whether you are communicating a request (hold palms out towards the other player/s), instructions (point a finger at the recipient) or idle gossip (use a hand to mime a mouth talking).

Thereafter the rules are as for normal charades—indicate the number of syllables you are miming and then attempt to use a mime to lead your co-workers to the correct sentence.

Work Space

If you shouted in space no one would be able to hear you even if they were right next to you.

Get the Job

Can you unscramble the anagram below to work out the job title?

He Let Rio

In the Calendar

What happened on December 29, 1170?

Unlikely Candidate

Opera singer

_____

Answers from previous page

The Filing Cabinet: Answer = Blackballed (contains only letters in the first half of the alphabet, the others contain only letters from the second half)
Who Am I? Answer = Elvis Costello
Words to Impress Your Colleagues: Hamose means hooked
Sing While You Work: Answer = *Work* Bob Marley

Email Word Association

This is an easy game that can occupy two or more workers for hours at a time.

The first player sends a single word email to the second player.

Second player reacts immediately with the word that comes to mind (for instance you might respond to "gate" with "field," "water," "community" or whatever). He or she adds this word to the top of the email and forwards, either to the original sender or to the next player in the ring.

The list continues to circulate as long as the players are bored enough to keep playing.

Along the way you may get some fascinating insights into your co-workers. Or you might just find a way to kill those difficult hours in the afternoon between lunchtime and the end of the working day.

Brief Survival Guide

Company merger:

Ignore new company name

Address only those in management from your original company

Resign...now!

Pick 'n' Mix

Choose 3 words to describe your work environment:

Poor	Minimal
Exclusive	Crazy
Arty	Filthy
Designer	Untidy
Disaster	Beautiful

Answers from previous page

In the Calendar: Answer = Archbishop Thomas Becket was murdered in Canterbury Cathedral

Get the Job: Answer = Hotelier